Processing Model of Conference Interpreting: Evaluation and Reconstruction

会议口译加工模式：评估与重构

任岳涛　著

全国百佳图书出版单位

图书在版编目（CIP）数据

会议口译加工模式：评估与重构/任岳涛著. —北京：知识产权出版社，2016.6
ISBN 978-7-5130-4000-6

Ⅰ.①会… Ⅱ.①任… Ⅲ.①会议—英语—口译—研究 Ⅳ.①H315.9

中国版本图书馆 CIP 数据核字（2016）第 003064 号

内容提要

会议口译是众多口译模式中对译员要求最高的一种。本书重新界定了会议口译定义及范围、延伸了口译过程，并在此基础上，对现有的口译加工模式进行评估与重构，推出了新的会议口译加工模式。重构的加工模式借用中国传统的"折扇"图形对会议口译的过程进行阐释。

责任编辑：刘晓庆　于晓菲　　　　　　　　　责任出版：孙婷婷

会议口译加工模式：评估与重构

HUIYI KOUYI JIAGONG MOSHI:PINGGU YU CHONGGOU

任岳涛　著

出版发行	知识产权出版社 有限责任公司	网　址：	http://www.ipph.cn	
电　话	010-82004826		http://www.laichushu.com	
社　址	北京市海淀区西外太平庄 55 号	邮　编：	100081	
责编电话	010-82000860 转 8363	责编邮箱：	yuxiaofei@cnipr.com	
发行电话	010-82000860 转 8101/8029	发行传真：	010-82000893/82003279	
印　刷	北京中献拓方科技发展有限公司	经　销：	各大网上书店、新华书店及相关专业书店	
开　本	787mm×1092mm　1/16	印　张：	9.5	
版　次	2016 年 6 月第 1 版	印　次：	2016 年 6 月第 1 次印刷	
字　数	120 千字	定　价：	42.00 元	

ISBN 978-7-5130-4000-6

出版权专有　侵权必究

如有印装质量问题，本社负责调换。

序（一）

任岳涛现在是河南省信阳师范学院的教师，主要讲授口译课程。他在河南大学外语学院攻读硕士学位时，是我指导的学生。他第一部独立完成的著作《会议口译加工模式：评估与重构》即将出版，请我写几句话。作为他的导师，我高兴之余，欣然应允。因为青年教师肯在学术领域努力钻研，是值得赞扬和鼓励的。

岳涛在学习期间，一致努力上进，成绩突出，尤其在口译实践与研究方面下了很大的功夫。实践上，他曾多次担任河南大学及省内外大型外事、商贸、文化、学术交流活动的翻译，在全国和河南省口笔译竞赛中赢得多次奖励，现在依然是活跃在中原地区的一名自由职业译员。在研究上，他是个有想法的年轻人。每次见面，他总是带着问题来，又带着新问题走，几天以后便有了自己的思路和见解。他还阅读了国内外不少口译方面的理论著作，从书后的参考文献可见一斑。

本书是他在硕士论文的基础上深化加工而成的。他的硕士论文毕业时获得了河南省优秀硕士论文奖，是河南省近年来少有的获得此奖励的外语类论文。通过进一步的加工修改，又有不小的提高。在本书中，岳涛努力消化其他学者的研究成果，根据自己的实践经历，总结和提出了一些新的见解和创新，如会议口译的定义、口译加工模式的衍变关系、口译过程的细化与延伸等。特别值得一提的是，对口译加工模式的重构，借用了中国传统文化中"折扇"的样式，虽然不尽完美，但却是一次冲破桎梏的尝试。

这些对当前越来越普遍的国际会议口译实践与研究都有一定的启发作用，对于一个刚走上学术研究之路的年轻人，无疑也是难能可贵和值得肯定的。

当然，作为年轻的作者，有些东西难免稚嫩。我相信经过磨砺，岳涛会在学术上逐步成熟的。

是为序。

郭尚兴

2016 年 3 月

于河南大学

序（二）

随着国际政治经济和社会交往日趋频繁，各种峰会、论坛等国际会议成为交往中的常用方式，对会议口译的需求和质量要求越来越高，与之伴随而来的就是国内逐渐升温的会议口译研究。

本书的研究基于释意学派口译理论，这符合该理论创始人塞莱斯科维奇的观点，即释意理论的研究对象为会议口译、意义。从释意学派的视角，口译是一种交际活动，其目的是传递意义。为了实现意义的充分传递，口译员须对源语话语进行释意；口译员在释意时需要进行认知补充，而认知补充是一个口译员的语言知识、主题知识、百科知识和语境知识相结合的过程。

针对会议口译，研究人员建立了不同层面的模型或模式，包括人类学层面、社会—职业层面、机构层面、互动层面、语篇层面、认知层面以及神经层面。会议口译的加工模式是一种认知层面的模式。目前具有代表性的加工模式多是建立在西方语言互译的基础之上，随着中西语互译的增多，中国的口译研究正在逐渐与世界接轨，口译研究的视域也在发生着转变。本书就是在这样的背景下，对已有的会议口译加工模式进行评估与重构。

本书的作者任岳涛是信阳师范学院外国语学院翻译专业的一名优秀青年

教师。作为翻译专业师资队伍的骨干力量，岳涛参加工作以来先后讲授了翻译硕士（MTI）的基础口译课程、翻译本科专业的英汉口译、汉英口译、交替传译、听译、听述、英语演讲与辩论和公共外交等课程；数次代表我院出任河南省翻译竞赛评审委员；担任着我院全国英语演讲比赛、辩论赛、师范生比赛以及翻译竞赛的指导教师工作，指导的学生多次获得国家级、省级奖励。

作为一名青年教师，岳涛在繁重的教学工作中还能抽出时间，将自己在口译教学与实践上的思考写下来，难能可贵。当他拿着书稿请我作序时，我欣然同意。一是对他在学术上的钻研精神表示肯定；二是希望鼓励更多的青年教师能够像岳涛一样，沉下心来，在做好教学工作的同时，潜心钻研学问，做到教学与科研相互促进。

刘世理

2016 年 3 月

于信阳师范学院

前　言

　　时光荏苒，十年前我进入河南大学，开始了在那里七年的学习生涯。从本科到研究生，这所百年名校在我的身上深深地烙上了"铁塔牌"的烙印。河南大学外语学院在外国语言文学研究方面可谓是众星云集、资源丰富。张今、吴雪莉、刘炳善、徐盛桓等几位先生是吾辈后学奋斗的榜样；学院几乎每周都有国内外专家的学术报告，"下课去听讲座"成了同学们常常挂在嘴边的话。得益于此，我才有机会广泛地学习了与翻译学相关的众多专业知识，如英美文学、跨文化交际、功能语法、转换生成语法、语篇分析、文体学及认知语言学等。这不仅印证了翻译所要求的"杂家"之说，也为我以后的学术研究打下了坚实的基础。

　　研究生时期，我师从郭尚兴教授，开始接触翻译及口译研究。在郭老师的指引下，我开始研读翻译学的主要经典著作，并选取了口译为自己硕士论文的研究方向。郭老师对我的论文要求极高，交给他的每一稿他都仔细审读并批改，甚至不惜让我对论文结构做颠覆式的调整。几经打磨，这部论文获得了评审专家的肯定，并获得了河南省优秀硕士论文的奖励。感谢郭老师的严格要求和谆谆教诲。

　　毕业后，我来到另一所高校任教，继续从事口译教学与研究。正是出于对口译由衷的热爱，我在原有硕士论文的基础上，结合工作以后的口译教学与实践经验，写出了这本拙著。在本书即将出版之际，请允许我向所有关心和支持我的人士致以由衷的谢意。

感谢河南大学外语学院翻译学博士生导师郭尚兴教授。感谢郭老师带我进入翻译学的殿堂，让我领略到翻译之美以及翻译学无穷的魅力。感谢郭老师在我研究的过程中给予的指导与鼓励。郭老师渊博的学识和严谨的治学态度对我的一生影响深远。

感谢信阳师范学院外国语学院院长刘世理教授。参加工作以来，刘老师一直关注我的教学和科研工作，并给予指导与引领。在本书的写作与出版过程中，刘老师更是给予了大力支持。

感谢河南大学外语学院我的老师：张克定教授、牛保义教授、刘辰诞教授、关合凤教授、杨朝军教授、姜玲教授、付江涛副教授、王晓伟博士和张晓辉老师，他们孜孜不倦的教诲令我受益终身。

感谢我的挚友同济大学外国语学院王磊博士、高等教育出版社汪于祺编辑、广东省人民政府外事办公室肖旭奕，以及对我给予支持和鼓励的同事、同行和朋友。感谢他们无私的启发、分享与帮助。

感谢知识产权出版社的于晓菲编辑和刘晓庆编辑在本书出版过程中所倾注的大量心血。

最后特别要感谢我的家人。感谢父母对我的教诲和支持，感谢妻子和女儿对我的理解、包容和鞭策，他们的幸福是我奋斗的不竭动力。

任岳涛

2016年3月

于信阳师范学院

Acknowledgements

In writing this book, I have received help from many people to whom I feel greatly indebted. First and foremost, I am very grateful to Professor Guo Shangxing, for his constructive advice and suggestions, his patient reading of my work, and his insightful comments. Without his guidance and encouragement, completing this book would have been almost impossible. He taught me a rigorous approach to academic research, one from which I shall benefit greatly throughout my life.

I would also like to thank Professor Liu Shili, Dean of the School of Foreign Languages at Xinyang Normal University, whose inspiring ideas and meticulous guidance aroused my interest in academic research.

I also offer my appreciation to the other professors with whom I have studies during my postgraduate career, including Professor Zhang Keding, Professor Niu Baoyi, Professor Liu Chendan, Professor Xu Youzhi, Professor Yang Chaojun, Professor Jiang Ling, Associate Professor Fu Jiangtao, Dr. Wang Xiaowei, and Mr. Zhang Xiaohui. Their excellent lectures helped me to acquire a comprehensive knowledge of translation and interpreting studies, linguistics and other related fields.

In the process of collecting the materials for this book and revising it, I was also fortunate to enjoy the support from my close friends Wang Lei, Wang Yuqi and Xiao Xuyi, who took the time to give me guidance and suggestions, even while busy working on their own projects. I would like to thank Ms. Yu Xiaofei, Ms. Liu Xiaoqing and Mr. Robert James, for their editing assistance, encouragement and patience.

Last but not least, I would like to express my thanks to my family, my wife Wang Saimei, and my friends, for their sincere love and deep concern.

Foreword

Interpretation and translation is one of the most rapidly-developing professions today. The emergence of China as the world's second-largest economic power has increased the need for accurate communication, and interpretation and translation are at the very core of this process. The many conferences, both regional and international, held to facilitate formal and in-person communication has led to increased demand for high-quality conference interpreting.

Conference interpreting research (CIR) in the West has long been an independent discipline, with a history spanning more than six decades; in China, however, CIR has been conducted for no more than two. Major CIR findings are often represented in the form of a model that can be divided into different levels——anthropological, socio-professional, institutional, interactional, textual, cognitive and neural. The processing model sits at the cognitive level, which reflects the nature of interpreting. However, most processing models are based on interpreting between Western languages. With the rise of China, interpreting between Eastern and Western languages has come to the center of interpreting studies in recent years, which has left space for the further study of processing models for conference interpreting.

Interpretive Theory is one of the predominant theories in CIR. Seleskovitch, founder of the Paris School and Interpretive Theory (IT), notes that the Paris School views interpreting as a communicative activity that aims at conveying the sense thereof, while IT focuses on conference interpreting and sense. To do so, the interpreter has to explain the source language, which often involves cognitive supplement, a process of fusing the interpreter's language knowledge, subject knowledge, encyclopedic knowledge and contextual knowledge. The Effort Models and the XiaDa Model are representatives of the processing model. Both portray interpreting as "explaining", that is, the interpreter interprets and conveys the sense of the communication, rather than the actual language. However, the two models were proposed nearly two decades ago, and can, to some degree, be refined to suit the changing demands of the developing market.

Contents

List of Abbreviations ··· 1

List of Figures ·· 2

Chapter One   Introduction ··· 3

1. 1 A Booming Industry ·· 3

1. 2 Models ·· 5

1. 3 Guide to the Contents of This Book ························ 6

Chapter Two   Conference Interpreting ····················· 8

2. 1 Interpreting ··· 8

2. 2 Conference Interpreting Revisited ··························· 16

2. 3 Processing Models of Conference Interpreting ······ 31

2. 4 Summary ·· 39

Chapter Three   The Interpretive Theory 41

3.1 Introduction 41

3.2 Key Concepts 47

3.3 IT and Processing Models of Conference Interpreting 59

3.4 Summary 59

Chapter Four   Evaluation of Processing Models of Conference Interpreting 61

4.1 Correlations 61

4.2 Comprehension 64

4.3 Analysis 67

4.4 Working Memory 69

4.5 Re-expression 72

4.6 Summary 73

Chapter Five   Reconstruction of the Processing Model of Conference Interpreting 75

5.1 Active Listening (AL) 75

5.2 Logical Analysis (LA) 91

5.3 Register Preparation (RP) 105

5.4 Knowledge Supplement (KS) 114

5.5 The Refined Processing Model for Conference Interpreting 120

5.6 Summary 122

Chapter Six   Conclusion 123

6.1 Major Findings 123

6.2 Limitations 126

6.3 Suggestions for Future Research 126

Bibliography 128

List of Abbreviations

1. AIIC: International Association of Conference Interpreters
2. CI: Consecutive Interpreting
3. CIAP: Conference Interpreters Asia Pacific
4. CIR: Conference Interpreting Research
5. EK: Encyclopedic Knowledge
6. EKL: Extra-linguistic Knowledge
7. ESIT: Ecole Supérieure d'Interprètes et de Traducteurs
8. KI: Knowledge Required for an Interpreter
9. KL: Knowledge for the Language
10. IT: Interpretive Theory
11. SCIC: Directorate General of Interpreting of the European Commission
12. SI: Simultaneous Interpreting

List of Figures

Figure 2. 1 The XiaDa Model for Interpreter Training

Figure 3. 1 Seleskovitch's Triangular Model (two versions)

Figure 5. 1 The Process of E-C Translation by Liu Miqing

Figure 5. 2 Interpersonal Communication Process by Gordon

Figure 5. 3 Active Listening by Gordon

Figure 5. 4 Information Hierarchy (IH) at sentence level

Figure 5. 5 Information Hierarchy (IH) at discourse level

Figure 5. 6 The Refined Processing Model of Conference Interpreting

Chapter One

Introduction

1.1 A Booming Industry

Interpretation and translation is one of the most rapidly-developing professions today. According to the China Foreign Language Administration, in 2015 there were 55,975 enterprises providing language services in China, 5,287 of which described translation and interpreting as their main services. According to IBISWorld, a market research company, translation and interpreting was a $33.5 billion industry in 2012, and is expected to grow to $37 billion by 2018. The U.S. Bureau of Labor Statistics (2012) has predicted a 46% growth in employment in the field by 2022, a conspicuously higher growth rate than in any other occupation.

In recent decades, China has become increasingly prominent on the global stage, in a wide range of areas: for example, Beijing hosted the 2008 Olympic Games, the 2010 World Expo was held in Shanghai, Chinese writer Mo Yan won the

Processing Model of Conference Interpreting: Evaluation and Reconstruction
会议口译加工模式：评估与重构

Nobel Prize in Literature in 2012, Chinese medical scientist Tu Youyou won the Nobel Prize in Physiology or Medicine 2015, and Beijing has been awarded the 2022 Winter Olympic Games. Over the past decade, China has expanded its horizons to include the world, and the world has undergone a period of reciprocal reformation and reconstruction. In the United States, for example, the Obama administration has proposed "pivoting" America's foreign affairs to focus on Asia, while Chinese President Xi Jinping has proposed a "new type of major power relationship" with the U.S. Accordingly, contacts and exchanges between the West and the East have increased exponentially, as has the demand for interpreters and translators. China's emergence as the world's second-largest economic power has also highlighted the growing need for accurate communications, with interpretation and translation being at the center of this process.

The most-advanced type of interpreting, conference interpreting, was first introduced at the 1919 Paris Peace Conference. It is a demanding and exacting profession, as the messages to be interpreted in a conference setting can be professional, encyclopedic, sophisticated or profound in nature. Conference interpreters not only pass messages, they also coordinate communication among participants, act as cultural consultants, and are participants in the communication itself. They must be able to listen, comprehend, memorize and transmit at almost the same time, often in the heat of debate.

Conference interpreting research (CIR) first began in the West in the 1930s; over the next eighty years CIR went through four developmental phases, and has nowbecome an independent discipline, albeit one that overlaps with many other subjects. In China CIR is a truly new discipline, having only begun in the mid-1990s. While CIR researchers use various models to represent their studies, the processing model is the most prevalent in China's CIR community, as it reflects the nature of interpreting and is often applied to interpreter training.

1.2 Models

Scientific research can be represented in the form of a model. For interpreting, modeling can be divided into different levels, including the anthropological, socio-professional, institutional, interactional, textual, cognitive and neural (Pöchhacker, 2004: 85–86). The processing model reflects the nature of interpreting, and addresses either general multi-task performance, or the specific processing stages and mental structures involved therein (Pöchhacker, 2004: 95–96). However, most existing processing models are based on interpreting Western languages, and models proposed by Chinese scholars do not receive much attention. In recent years, interpreting between Western and Eastern languages (mostly between European languages and Asian/Arabic languages) has come to the center of interpreting studies. Thus, the author has chosen the processing model of conference interpreting as this book's research subject.

By evaluating and reconstructing the processing model, the author of this book intends to answer the following questions:

1) What are the relationships between previous processing models?

2) To what degree are the components of these models applicable to interpreting between Eastern and Western languages?

3) What other components have been incorporated as refinements to reflect the nature of interpreting between Eastern and Western languages?

Questions 1) and 2) involve evaluating previous processing models for conference interpreting. Question 3) tries to reconstruct the processing model from an Interpretive Theory perspective, so as to reflect the nature of conference interpreting in the new era.

1.3 Guide to the Contents of This Book

This book consists of six chapters.

Chapter One is an introduction to the research background, the research questions, the significance of the research and the organization of the book.

Chapter Two introduces interpreting, conference interpreting and processing models of conference interpreting. Based on a review of previous studies, the author proposes a working definition for conference interpreting that forms the basis of this book.

Chapter Three introduces the origin, development and achievements of Interpretive Theory, and elaborates on the key concepts thereof, including deverbalization, the triangular model and the interpreter training model. Interpretive Theory is a predominant theory that has been applied to both translation and interpreting studies; as it shares the same target as the processing models, it is used as this book's theoretical foundation.

Chapter Four is an evaluation of processing models for conference interpreting, from two perspectives—an examination of the correlations among processing models (i. e.. the development of and relations between these models), and a detailed evaluation of their major components.

Chapter Five reconstructs the processing model of conference interpreting, based on components derived from the evaluation of previous models with the aim of refining them to form a cohesive processing model of conference interpreting.

Chapter Six concludes the research, discusses its major findings and limitations, and offers suggestions for future research.

Chapter Two

Conference Interpreting

2.1 Interpreting

2.1.1 History

Interpreting came into being when migration brought humans from different areas or groups into contact, and the barriers to communication caused by language differences were discovered. Those who grew up in a bilingual environment and who could speak two or more languages naturally became the facilitators of communications and exchanges between people from different cultures. Since interpreting is a verbal form of translation, it is difficult to find written proof of its creation and evolution, or to pinpoint when it was created. The first written proof of interpreting dates back to 3000 BC, when the ancient Egyptians had a hieroglyphic signifying "interpreter" (Delisle, 1999: 22). In ancient China, interpreters were called *Ji* (寄) in the east, *Didi* (狄鞮) in the west, *Xiang* (象) in the south, and *Yi* (译) in the north (黎难秋, 2002: 5).

The next stage in the evolution of interpreting was occasioned by the ancient Greeks and Romans, who felt it undignified to learn the language of a conquered people themselves, and so forced slaves, prisoners and ethnic hybrids to learn multiple languages and interpret for the patrician class. From the Roman era up until the 17th century, Latin was the Western world's lingua franca (i. e., a bridge language that allows communication between people without a shared native language or dialect) and the language of diplomacy and education in Europe; every country had to have some people who spoke Latin, if only to allow diplomatic relations. The word "interpreter" came from the Latin *interpres*, meaning one who explains or translates.

Around the turn of the 20th century, interpreting first began to be used in international meetings, and it was at the end of the First World War, during the 1919 Paris Peace Conference, when consecutive interpreting was first used officially. This marked the beginning of modern interpreting, and established conference interpreting, and many other types of interpreting, as a profession.

The first attempt to introduce simultaneous interpreting was made before the Second World War, at the International Labor Conference in Geneva, Switzerland, in 1927. However, due to its cost and a lack of facilities, simultaneous interpreting was not used on a large scale until the Nuremberg war crimes trials, in 1945. Before that, consecutive interpreting was widely used in international conferences, as the language of world diplomacy was then still bound to French and English. In 1947, UN Resolution 152 established simultaneous interpreting as a permanent service for the United Nations.

In 1953, the first professional organization for conference interpreters, the International Association of Conference Interpreters (AIIC) was founded. The AIIC is the largest and most widely recognized global association of conference interpreters, and membership therein signifies an interpreter's professional stature and experience. The founding of the AIIC was a milestone in the professionalization of modern interpreting.

Interpreting, as a profession, has been growing rapidly ever since, with research institutions and interpreter training programs set up in over 70 countries or regions across the world, according to the American Translator Association.❶ The size of the industry was $33.5 billion in 2012 and is projected to reach $37 billion in 2018, according to IBISWorld❷, a market research company.

2.1.2 Classifications

Interpreting can be classified into different groups, based on such dimensions as working mode, interpreting task or setting, and interpreting direction. Although not an exhaustive list, the working modes most frequently encountered in interpreting studies are *consecutive*, *simultaneous*, *whispered*, and *relay interpreting*.

In consecutive interpretation, the interpreter does not speak until the original speaker has stopped, and therefore has time to analyze the message as a whole and understand its overall meaning; the interpreter is in the room and speaks to the lis-

---

❶ http://www.atanet.org/certification/eligibility_approved.php#top
❷ http://media.ibisworld.com/2013/10/22/top-performing-service-industries/

teners face-to-face, effectively becoming the speaker (Seleskovitch, 1978: 123). In simultaneous interpretation, the interpreter is located in a booth away from the parties, and speaks at the same time as the speaker; as such, the interpreter has no need to memorize or jot down what has been said, and the analysis-comprehension and reconstruction-expression processes are telescoped. The interpreter works on the message bit by bit, passing on the portion he has understood while analyzing and assimilating the next idea (Seleskovitch, 1978: 125).

Whispered interpreting takes place when simultaneous interpretation equipment is not available, and involves simultaneously interpreting a speaker's comments and whispering them into the ear of the one or, at most, two others (Jones, 1998: 6). Relay interpreting is usually used in situations involving several target languages. A source-language interpreter interprets the text into a language common to every interpreter, each of whom then renders the message to their respective target languages. In heavily multilingual meetings, there may be more than one "intermediate" language. For example, a Greek source language could be interpreted into English and thence to other languages; at the same time, it may also be directly interpreted into French, and from French into yet more languages. This solution is often used in EU institutions' multilingual meetings.❶

In terms of interpreting tasks or settings, interpreting can be categorized as either conference, court, community, escort, media, medical or business interpreting.

According to the Conference Interpreters Asia Pacific (CIAP) organization,

---

❶ http://en.wikipedia.org/wiki/Language_interpretation#Relay

conference interpretation is the simultaneous or consecutive rendering of a speech at a conference in a language or cultural setting that is different than the original.❶ Most conferences involve simultaneous interpreting, although interpreters must be prepared to perform in the consecutive mode as well (Jones, 1998: 7). Some writers have equated conference interpreting with simultaneous interpreting or interpreting, which may result in some confusion surrounding the notions; this book distinguishes between these notions.

Court interpreting, also referred to as legal, judicial or forensic interpreting, refers to interpretation that takes place in a legal setting, such as a courtroom or an attorney's office, wherein some proceeding or activity related to law is conducted (Gonzalez, et al, 1991: 25). Community Interpreting enables people who are not fluent speakers of a country's official language (s) to communicate with public service providers, to facilitate the speaker's full and equal access to legal, health, education, government, and social services. (Carr, et al, 1995) The community interpreter's role and responsibilities are very different from those of a commercial or conference interpreter; as he/she must enable mutually satisfactory communication between professional and client, despite their very different backgrounds and perceptions, and their unequal power and knowledge.❷

In escort interpreting, the interpreter accompanies people requiring interpreting services to social or cultural events—e. g., guided tours, factory visits, city tourism,

---

❶ http: //www. ciap. net/index. php? option=com_ content&view=article&id=81&Itemid=82
❷ http: //aiic. net/page/234

formal dinners, etc. —at which a language not known by the client is spoken. Escort interpretation is most often consecutive, and is usually limited to a few sentences at a time (Gonzalez, et al, 1991: 28).

By its very nature, media interpreting has to be conducted in simultaneous mode. It is commonly provided during live television coverage of such events as press conferences and presidential campaigns, and during live or taped interviews with political figures, entrepreneurs, artists, sportsmen or newsmakers. A media interpreter sits in a sound-proof booth, and ideally can see the speakers on a monitor or on the set. Media interpreting is more stressful than other types of interpreting, as the interpreter must overcome a wide range of technical problems associated with control room hassles and wrangling during live coverage, while still sounding as slick and confident as a television presenter.❶

Medical interpreting, also referred to as health care interpreting or hospital interpreting, encompasses a variety of medical settings and situations, from routine consultations with a physician to emergency procedures, and from pre-planned childbirth classes to supporting complex laboratory testing (Frishberg, 1986: 115). Business interpreting (or trade or commercial interpreting) typically occurs among a few individuals, mostly during smaller scale private business dealings, but also in other business-related scenarios, e. g., interviews, seminars, workshops, negotiations, factory visits, telephone conferences and so on. While business interpreting is commonly either consecutive or simultaneous, whispering and telephone interpreting is

---

❶ http://en.wikipedia.org/wiki/Language_interpretation#Media

also used, depending on the circumstances.❶

In regard to direction, interpreting can be divided into two types: one-way interpreting (which transfers language B to language A in a single direction), and two-way interpreting (which transfers language B to language A, and language A to language B at the same time). The latter is more challenging due to language A to language B command imbalance. At the United Nations, two-way interpreting is confined to Chinese and Arabic languages.

It should be noted that the above classifications and perspectives have some overlap. Live coverage of the most recent U.S. presidential election, for example, was interpreted on major TV channels and on the Internet. From a taskor setting perspective, this was an example of media interpreting; in terms of working mode, however, it was simultaneous interpreting.

2.1.3 Features

Translation, in general, is a complex communicative activity that involves two languages. Compared with written translation, interpreting has several unique features.

Firstly, interpreting differs from translation in terms of their origin of respective names. The English word "interpreter" derives from the Latin *interpres*, meaning "one who explains," while "translate" derives from the Latin *translatus*, meaning "to carry across"; thus, to translate is not to explain, but to switch from one

---

❶ http://www.tjc-global.co.uk/?pid=business_interpreting&lang=en

language to another.

Secondly, unlike translation, interpreting is a real-time process in which the interpreter must ensure fluent communication between parties without hesitating or taking time to think. Unlike a translator, who can consult a dictionary or an expert when facing difficulties, the interpreter has to finish his/her task alone and within seconds; thus nervousness is common among interpreters, experienced or not.

Thirdly, interpreting and translation differ in terms of their language features. Interpreting employs oral language, which differs from written language in terms of phonetics, grammar, word choice and sentence structure. Thus, an interpreter must understand accurately the speaker's intention based on their vocal stresses, intonations, body language and facial expressions (吴冰, 1995: III), while simultaneously coping with the speaker's accent and speed of speech. At the same time, the interpreter must be a good speaker, with clear and accurate pronunciation, and organized and logical expression, so as to make the speaker's intention understood to the listener.

As interpreting differs from translation, so too does the study of interpreting differ from that of translation. This difference should be emphasized in the study of conference interpreting. A conference may involve some written materials that relate, directly or indirectly, to the speaker's speech, such as supporting documents, drafts, or a copy of the speech to be interpreted. However, these materials are merely an aid to the interpreter, for whom listening is the primary source of the message to be interpreted; putting the interpreter's words into written form or comparing them with the original text is meaningless. As the AIIC notes, conference interpretation is an oral intellectual exercise, and quite distinct from drafting a written text, as there is no known instance of a spoken language being completely transferable into acceptable written form; as such, any attempt to put transcribe the recorded content of a conference interpretation, without considerable preliminary editing by professional minute takers or translators, can only yield questionable results.❶

2.2 Conference Interpreting Revisited

2.2.1 Definition

As the most demanding type of interpreting, conference interpreting has received great attention from the CIR community. Although conference interpreting has some common grounds with other types of interpreting, it has its own unique features. Researchers, interpreters, teachers and professional organizations offer various definitions of this profession.

From a researcher's perspective, conference interpreters may be prototypically characterized as people who have skills in consecutive and simultaneous interpreting, who interpret at important meetings (technical, political, scientific or other), who are expected to meet high quality standards, and who consider themselves to be a part of the conference interpreting community (Gile, 2006). More specifically, Robin Setton (1994: 55) has argued that conference interpreting involves "under-

---

❶ http://aiic.net/page/58

standing a speech event expressed in one human language and producing another 'similar' speech act using a different language and for a specific audience, either 1) simultaneously, or 2) consecutively, i. e., while the speaker pauses or after he/she has finished".

Second, from the perspective of professional organizations, the AIIC (the largest recognized professional organization for conference interpreters) depicts a conference interpreter as "a professional language and communication expert who, at multilingual meetings, conveys the meaning of a speaker's message orally and in another language to listeners who would not otherwise understand", usually working from one or more foreign languages into their mother tongue. It points out that conference interpreters use different modes of interpretation (simultaneous, consecutive, whispering), depending on the type of meeting and working environment, and usually work as part of a team assembled for a specific conference by a consultant interpreter, taking into account the event's language needs and other requirements. According to the AIIC, interpreters are committed to quality and professionalism, are bound by a code of professional ethics, and observe the strictest professional secrecy; moreover, a conference interpreter's work is an oral intellectual exercise quite distinct from written translation and requires different training and qualifications.[1] According to Conference Interpreters Asia Pacific (CIAP), a regional organization for interpreters, conference interpreting is "the rendering of a speech at a conference in a different language and cultural setting than the original. It can be

---

[1] http://aiic.net/page/1469

simultaneous or consecutive. It is different from community interpreting, escort interpreting, business interpreting, etc". ❶

Third, from the perspective of government and institutions, the European Commission's Directorate General of Interpreting (SCIC), the largest official employer of conference interpreters in Europe, defines conference interpreting as dealing "exclusively with oral communication: rendering a message from one language into another, naturally and fluently, adopting the delivery, tone and convictions of the speaker and speaking in the first person". ❷ International conferences are attended by people from different backgrounds and cultures, and speaking different languages; the SCIC holds that it is the job of an interpreter to enable them to communicate with each other—not by translating every word they utter, but by conveying the ideas they seek to express (ibid).

Based on the above perspectives, conference interpreting has its own features, which distinct it from other types of interpreting. Two key features include the ability to deal appropriately with massive amounts of information, and a command of formal and written language.

Regarding the former, conferences and meetings usually have a set *topic*, which can vary greatly depending on the conference's nature (e. g., agricultural, scientific, industrial, military, medical, cultural, etc.); different topics involve different terms and registers. It is common for a speech to include a lot of numbers or proper names

---

❶ http://ciap.net/index.php?option=com_content&view=article&id=81&Itemid=82
❷ http://ec.europa.eu/dgs/scic/what-is-conference-interpreting/index_en.htm

within relatively few sentences. Conference interpreters must not only understand this data and the logic behind it, but also store them in their working memory, and then reorganize and re-express them into the target language. A good command of both linguistic and extra-linguistic knowledge is therefore necessary.

A command of formal and written language is key, as speakers usually prepare their speeches ahead of time, generally using more formal words, longer and more complex sentence structures, and a written form of language, which causes them to speak in longer segments than they would in their normal daily conversations; moreover, although conference interpreters can sometimes get a copy of a speech's script or major contents before it is delivered, they still must deal with digressions and unexpected situations on the spot. The speaker may also use professional terms and expressions specific to their field, which may be difficult for the interpreter to understand and to express in another language. The speaker might cite a saying, coin a new word or expression on the spot, or mention proper names unexpectedly, for none of which could the interpreter be prepared; thus, conference interpreters need to have a strong and clear mind to enable them to face unpredictable situations.

It must be remembered that conference interpreters render messages, not words, and that their job is quite distinct from that of translators. Their primary responsibility is to facilitate communication among delegates and speakers at international conferences within the bounds of their code of professional ethics. Although conference interpreting overlaps with other types of interpreting, it is much more difficult and unpredictable and requires higher quality standards; thus, to become a qualified conference interpreter, professional training is necessary.

Hu Gengshen (2000) differentiated nine kinds of CONFERENCE—meetings, conferences, symposia, congresses, conventions, fora, seminars, workshops and colloquia. For Hu, meeting is a general and summary term for various kinds of assemble ages of people who are gathered together for a particular purpose, whereas a conference is a more formal meeting that centers on a specialized professional or academic event, and at which formal discussions take place, often over a period of several days. A conference may include formal and informal meetings, visual and audio presentations, teaching, consultations, exhibitions, business talks, visits, and other social activities. A symposium is a kind of meeting for specialized academic discussion; it is usually narrower and more specific, in terms of its range of topics, than is a conference. The basic characteristic of a congress is that it is usually attended by representatives or delegates belonging to national or international, governmental or non-governmental organizations, and is held to discuss issues, ideas, and policies of public interest. It is usually large in scale and generally representative and extensive.

A convention is a kind of routine meeting at which large numbers of people gather to meet and discuss business specific to their organization or political group; conventions are regularly organized by learned societies, professional associations, academic institutions, or NGOs. A forum is a public meeting at which people exchange ideas and discuss issues, especially important public issues. Seminars are class-like meetings at which participants discuss a particular topic or subject that has been presented by one or more major speakers. A seminar can take the form of a lecture, followed by a related discussion. A workshop is a period of discussion or practical work that involves a group of people learning about a given subject by sharing their knowledge or experience on a particular subject, and may include such relevant activities as demonstrations, displays and operations during the course of presentation. Finally, a colloquium is a more formal sort of academic seminar, one that is usually larger and that involves panel discussions at which invited experts or professionals in a particular field express their ideas and opinions around a specific topic (胡庚申, 2000: 1-4; 5-8).

These nine variations, when organized at the international level and interpreters arranged, are generically referred to as CONFERENCE in interpreting studies, and the interpreters there at as CONFERENCE INTERPRETERS. Given that activities at the various forms of conference are rather inclusive, conference interpreting, as a profession, overlaps with such other types of interpreting as escort interpreting, media interpreting and business interpreting etc. Therefore, in CIR, both INTERPRETER and CONFERENCE INTERPRETER are used to refer to conference interpreter.

From the above, conference and conference interpreting can be seen to have the following features:

1. Conference is an activity through which people gather to exchange ideas and discuss certain issues;

2. Information may be exchanged at a conference in both written (documents, PPT, handouts, etc.) and oral form (speech, panel discussion or interview, etc.);

3. When a conference is at regional or international level and involves more than one working language, conference interpreters will be a part of the conference; and,

4. The aim of conference interpreting is to facilitate communication at various conference activities.

Thus, interpreting for speeches, presentations, bilateral or multilateral talks, exhibitions, business negotiations, visits, tours, media conferencesand interviews all fall within the scope of the study of CONFERENCE INTERPRETING.

Based on the above discussions, the author proposes the following working definition of conference interpreting.

Conference interpreting is a type of interpreting performed at international or inter- lingual conferences to facilitate proper communication at all conference activities. Conference interpreting is an inclusive job that, although its functions overlap with those of other types of interpreting (court, business, community, etc.), requires higher quality standards, and has strict code of professional ethics.

2.2.2 Working Modes

In the West, simultaneous interpreting is the dominant working mode for conference interpreters. In China, due to a lack of interpreting equipment (booths, interpreter consoles, mixers, transmission systems, headset receivers and microphones), consecutive interpreting is also widely used; whispering, relay and liaison interpreting modes are also applied in certain situations. The AIIC has explained, in detail, how interpreters work❶:

---

❶ http://aiic.net/node/7/how-interpreters-work

In simultaneous interpreting, the interpreter sits in a booth, listens to the speaker in one language through headphones, and immediately speaks their interpretation into a microphone in another language, transmitting it to the headphones of the listeners in the meeting room. Simultaneous interpretation is appropriate in bilingual or multilingual meetings and has the advantages of not lengthening the meeting, encouraging lively discussion, and eliciting spontaneous contributions. Simultaneous interpretation requires a high level of concentration, as the interpreter is doing several things at once; interpreters therefore perform their duties in turns of about 30 minutes each.

During consecutive interpreting, the interpreter is in the same room as the speaker and follows their speech while taking notes, before presenting their interpretation. Very long speeches may be broken up into parts, with interpretation following each part; however, a trained interpreter is capable of providing consecutive interpretation for speeches several minutes in length. This kind of interpretation is more suitable for scientific and technical presentations given by a single speaker, or meetings at which only a small number of languages are spoken, as it makes the meeting longer. Note-taking is an essential part of consecutive interpreting, but involves committing the logic and structure of a statement to paper as a memory aid, rather than recording everything that is said.

Whispered interpreting is essentially simultaneous interpreting without a booth or interpreting equipment. At least two interpreters take turns sitting very close to the listeners and providing simultaneous interpretation *sotto voce*. The practice is hard on the voice, appropriate only for short meetings, and is not recommended for more than two listeners.

By comparison, the SCIC lists nine modes for its conference interpreters[1], some of which (consecutive, simultaneous and whisper) overlap with the AIIC categories. The other six (relay, retour, pivot, cheval, asymmetric and sign language) can be described as follows:

1. Relay interpreting involves interpreting between two languages via a third. When a delegate speaks in a language not covered by an interpreter in an active language booth, the interpreter can connect, via audio link, to an interpreter in another booth who does cover that language, and relay the results thereof without perceptible loss of quality.

2. Retour (from the French for "to return") is a universally applied term describing the practice of working from your mother tongue into a foreign language. Although interpreters normally work into their mother tongue, some interpreters know a second language well enough to be able to work into that language from their mother tongue. Retour interpreting is especially useful for providing relays from lesser-to better-known languages.

3. Pivot interpreting involves using a single language as a relay.

4. Cheval mode refers to an interpreter alternatively working into two languages in a single meeting.

5. In asymmetric interpreting, all delegates speak in their mother tongue, but

---

[1] http://ec.europa.eu/dgs/scic/what-is-conference-interpreting/index_en.htm

interpretation thereof is available in only a few languages. Naturally, for asymmetric interpretation to be feasible, all delegates must understand one or more of the active languages.

6. Sign language interpreters work in meetings with deaf participants and provide simultaneous interpretation from spoken language into signed language and back. The interpreter sits or stands, clearly visible, in front of the deaf delegates.

Since some of these working modes partly overlap, only the dominant modes, consecutive and simultaneous interpreting, fall within the scope of this study.

2.2.3 Conference Interpreting Research (CIR)

The first study into conference interpreting was conducted in 1931, when Spanish psychologist Jesús Sanz published a study on the work and abilities of conference interpreters (Pöchhacker, 2004); the study was, however, an isolated instance (Gile, 2006), and it was not until the publication of two classic studies-Jean Herbert's *Manuel de l'interprète* (1952) and Jean-François Rozan's *La prise de notes en consécutive* (1956) that CIR truly began. CIR in the West can be divided into four periods: Pre-research; Experimental Psychology; Practitioners; and Renewal (肖晓燕, 2002).

CIR's Pre-research Period, from the 1950s to the 1960s, focused on the individual experiences of interpreters, as well as their observations of and reflections on interpreting and their working environment. Major topics during this period were language and knowledge requirements for interpreters, difficulties interpreters might face, the interpreter-client relationship, and factors affecting target language production. Although CIR in this period lacked a theoretical foundation, Herbert's and Rozan's two works are nonetheless considered the classics in the field, and their principles for note-taking in consecutive interpreting are still applied by a majority of interpreters worldwide (Gile, 2006).

The second period, from the 1960s to the early 1970s, was CIR's Experimental Psychology Period, in which researchers focused on cognitive issues, based on a theoretical framework drawn from psychology and psycholinguistics. Researchers, mainly cognitive psychologists and psycholinguists (Oléron and Nanpon, Goldman-Eisler, Barik, Gerver), hypothesized about the interpreting process, and analyzed the impact of such variables as the source language, noise, speakers' speaking speed, and EVS (Ear-Voice Span), among others, on interpreting, and how interpreters coped with those variables. Gerver, the most active of these researchers, conducted experiments on interpretation over a period of 10 years, and co-organized, with Sinaiko (1978), a symposium on interpretation that brought together interpreters and scientists from various disciplines to initiate research cooperation; unfortunately, there was no follow up to this initiative (Gile, 1994). Gerver is often called a pioneer in the *information-processing paradigm in the field*; however, since the researchers in this period were not interpreters themselves, there is doubt as to whether their research helped people better understand the interpreting process.

The third period, from the early 1970s to the mid-1980s, was the Practitioners Period. The 1977 conference organized by Gerver and Sinaiko may be taken, symbolically, as the point at which research in the field began to be taken over by interpreting practitioners, who chose to ignore their predecessors' methods and findings both (as reflected by an almost total absence of citations of their studies in the literature), instead pursuing their own mode of investigation (Gile, 2006). CIR in this period was dominated by Danica Seleskovitch, at the Ecole Supérieure d'Interprètes et de Traducteurs (ESIT) of the Université Paris III. Her research centered on her *théorie du sens* (theory of sense), also known as the Interpretive Theory (IT), which essentially postulates total deverbalization between comprehension of the source speech and production of the target speech by the interpreter, denies language-pair-specific processes, and ignores linguistic and cognitive difficulties (Gile, 2006). Seleskovitch has supervised many papers and more than 10 doctoral dissertations on interpreting, and written or contributed to several books and many papers. ESIT became a source of inspiration to aspiring interpreting researchers in the West (Gile, 2006). During this period, several models of interpreting were developed, including information-processing-oriented ones (Moser 1978, Gerver 1976) and Gile's processing-capacity-oriented "Effort-Model" (Gile, 1995), and several ideas were formed on training, processes, the differences between interpretation of ad-libbed speeches and speeches read from texts, and other aspects of interpreting.

The fourth (and current) period (the Renewal Period; also called the "Renaissance") (Gile, 1994), dates from the late 1980s—specifically, a conference on interpreter training organized by the Translation and Interpreting School (SSLMIT) of the University of Trieste in November, 1986. During this conference, scholars challenged numerous aspects of the prevailing CIR dogma (Gran and Dodds, 1989), and called for an interdisciplinary approach involving more cooperation with researchers from other fields. More empirical studies have been conducted during this period and many research centers founded around the world, with ESIT being the leading one.

Generally speaking, CIR in the West has five main characteristics. First, most of the research is done by practicing interpreters; however, these researchers increasingly attempt to use findings and ideas from studies on written translation and from the cognitive sciences, conduct cooperative projects with scientists from other disciplines, and calls for more cooperation with experts outside the field.

Second, there is an increasing emphasis in empirical studies, the number of which has increased dramatically over the past few years.

Third, there is increased communication between interpretation researchers, as can be seen in the Trieste school's journal, *The Interpreter's Newsletter*, the AIIC's efforts (through its Research Committee) to compile and update an interpretation bibliography, ISIT's creation of an international network for information on interpretation research (IRTIN) in Paris, the opening up of former East Block countries, and China's willingness to invite researchers from the West to speak at its National Symposium on Interpreting.

Fourth, the movement has been accompanied by a more open-minded attitude on the part of practicing researchers, more due to the larger number and impact of "second generation researchers" whose attitudes differ from those of their elders, than to changes in the latter's position. For example, while research activity in Trieste, Vienna, Brisbane and Tokyo has over the past five years or so, ESIT has kept a low profile, and has published very few research papers (Gile, 1994).

Fifth, while most Western researchers focus on five issues (interpreting training, language issues, cognitive issues, quality issues, and professionalism), the models they have put forward are not sufficiently comprehensive. For instance, Seleskovitch's (1984) Triangular Model concerns the information-processing process of interpreting, while Gile's (1995) Effort Model deals with how simultaneous interpreters handle more than one task at the same time.

CIR in China began in the mid-1990s, its development symbolized successive iterations of the country's National Symposium on Interpreting. CIR in China can be divided into three stages: the Primary Research period; the Theoretical Research period; and the Professionalized research period.

The Primary Research period lasted from 1996 to 2000, during which two national symposiums on interpreting were organized; the first of these, the National Symposium on Interpreting Theories and Teaching, was convened in Xiamen in 1996 and mostly covered topics related to problems in interpreter training. During this period, CIR in China could not really be called that—it was only a preliminary probe into interpreting and interpreter training.

From 2000 to 2003 was the The oretical Research Period, during which researchers began to study interpreting from an interdisciplinary perspective, and to focus on the assessment of interpreting quality. China's fourth national symposium, an international event set in Beijing, was conducted during this period, and provided a platform for international academic communication. During this period, Chinese researchers began to focus on theoretical studies on interpreting; since conference interpreting is the dominant type of interpreting worldwide, China gradually became a member of the global CIR community.

From 2004 on marks the Professionalized Research Period. China's fifth symposium (held during this period) centered on issues of professionalism in interpreting. Experts from AIIC, ESIT and other international organizations discussed, with Chinese researchers, issues related to increased demand for interpreting services, and called for market standardization. To that end, they discussed professional training for interpreting skills, including relevant course arrangements, teaching methods and training materials. Delegates at China's seventh symposium, in 2008, discussed the future of and challenges to interpreting in China, including curriculum, teacher development and interpreting teaching models. By that time, some universities in China had already begun to offer MTI (Master of Translation and Interpreting) and BTI (Bachelor of Translation and Interpreting) programs; by 2015, according to China's Foreign Language Administration, 196 universities in China had offered BTI programs and 206 universities had offered MTI programs.

In Chinese CIR, *most research work is done by university teachers*, and centers on theoretical studies, practical skills and techniques, or teaching and training. Methodological issues have becoming the concern of more and more researchers, who have begun to compare their own studies to practices in the West. However, since most researchers are college teachers, rather than conference interpreters, many do not have a clear understanding of the distinctions between conference interpreting and other types of interpreting. As such, their research is more accurately described as interpreting research in general, rather than CIR.

CIR has long been an independent discipline in the West, with more than fifty years of history, while CIR has been a research area in China for barely a decade. However, the conference interpreting models put forward by Western and Chinese researchers alike have not been updated in the past decade, despite the growing interpreting market in China. This points to a need for further comprehensive study of conference interpreting models.

2.3 Processing Models of Conference Interpreting

A model can be described as a form of representation of an object or phenomenon (Pöchhacker, 2004: 84). Processing models for conference interpreting address issues like multiple task performance in general, specific processing stages, mental structures involved, as well as the nature of the translational process (Pöchhacker, 2004: 95-96). The most influential processing models for conference interpreting are the Effort Models, and the XiaDa model.

2.3.1 The Effort Models

The Effort Models, proposed by Daniel Gile, a professor of translation at the Université Lyon 2, France, are dominant in Western countries. In 1985, Gile identified three basic efforts needed for simultaneous interpreting—L (Listening and Analysis), M (Memory), and P (Production) —and claimed that "there is only a limited amount of mental 'energy' (or processing capacity) available for the interpreter's processing effort, and that the sum of the three efforts must not exceed the interpreter's processing capacity" (Gile, 1985), such that:

(L + P + M) < Capacity

In his book *Basic Concepts and Models for Interpreter and Translator Training* (Gile, 1995), Gile refined this model by adding C (Coordination Effort) in his studies of consecutive and simultaneous interpreting, such that the model for simultaneous interpreting is:

SI = L + M + P + C

Where SI stands for Simultaneous Interpreting; L for Listening and Analysis; M for Short-term Memory Effort; P for Speech Production; and C for Coordination. Gile divides consecutive interpreting into two phases. The model for Phase I is:

CI = L + N + M + C

Where CI stands for Consecutive Interpreting; L for Listening and Analysis; N for Note-taking; M for Short-term Memory Effort; and C for Coordination, while the Phase II model is:

CI = Rem + Read + P

Where CI stands for Consecutive Interpreting; Rem for Remembering, Read for Note-reading; and P for Production.

These two models for SI and CI are "models of operational constraints, not architectural models, insofar as they do not postulate a particular mental structure and information-processing flow like the other models do" (Gile, 1995: 94). More important, they are built on the basis of the interpreting process (comprehension-deverbalization-reproduction) found in IT. Gile also put forward an equation emphasizing the importance of comprehension in interpreting (Gile, 1995: 80):

C = KL + EKL + A

Where C stands for Comprehension; KL for Knowledge for the Language; EKL for Extra-linguistic Knowledge; and A for Analysis.

In these equations " = " does not imply actual equality; rather, it refers to the result of the interaction among the components of the equation. Similarly, " + " refers to addition through interaction, rather than to purely arithmetic addition.

2.3.2 The XiaDa Model

CIR in China is in a growing stage, one in which new principles and models are being built that take Chinese culture and language into consideration. Huge differences in terms of both language and culture exist between the East and the West, and have become major problems for conference interpreters. The XiaDa Model for Interpreter Training, by Lin Yuru (Xiamen University, China) and Jack Lonergan (University of Westminster, UK), is based on Gile's earlier work in response to these circumstances. The word "XiaDa" is an abbreviated Chinese *pinyin* for Xiamen University, which is located in Fujian Province in southeast China.

In their book, *Interpreting for Tomorrow* (《新编英语口译教程》)（林郁如, 1999）, Lin and Longeran asserted their belief that, while Gile has emphasized the importance of comprehension in interpretation, "comprehension alone is not enough to enable interpretation. The interpreter needs to comprehend, but then to reproduce the message contents in the target language applying the skills and techniques of interpreters. The result must also conform to professional standards and ethics" (林郁如, 1999: xxi-xxii). Accordingly, they amended Gile's formula as follows:

I = S + C + P

Where "I stands for the act of successful interpreting. S refers to the skills and techniques involved in interpreting what is comprehended. C stands for comprehension as described by Gile, and P suggests that the whole is carried out to a professional standard" (林郁如, 1999: xxii).

Lin and Lonergan argued that, while "much of Gile's account is relevant to high-level conference interpreting, at the level of European Union meetings", many interpreters' work "might well be primarily in business or commerce. Day-to-day interpreting is far removed from the specialist conditions associated with several members of an interpreting team occupying a booth at an international conference, with prepared documentation to hand" (林郁如, 1999: xxii). Taking Gile's analytical ideas a step further resulted in the XiaDa Model for Interpreter Training (Figure 2.1).

According to its creators, the XiaDa model, while rather macro in perspective, "is a non-linear approach. Its main aim is to show that interpreting requires comprehension of the SL and reconstruction of the message in the TL. Furthermore, this is made possible by an analysis of the discourse and cultural factors in the scenario, and all is undertaken using the skills and professionalism of interpreters" (林郁如, 1999: xxiii-xxiv). As it is shown in the above figure, S (Skills and Techniques) and P (Professional standards and Ethics) lie at the center of the XiaDa Model, and are key components thereof. As the earliest interpreting training model designed in

China, this model has been widely received by the CIR community in China.

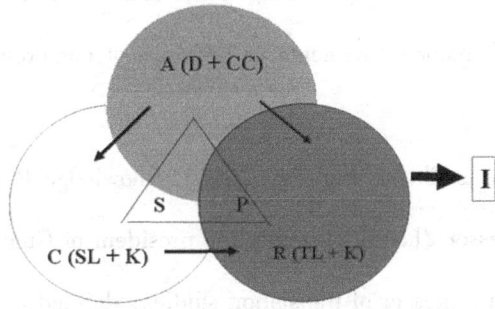

Figure 2.1   The XiaDa Model for Interpreter Training[1]

2.3.3 Refinements of the Processing Models

As mentioned in the previous discussion, some CIR researchers are also inter-

---

[1] Key to Xiada Model: (林郁如, 1999: xxiv-xxvii)
C (SL+K) represents comprehension (C) of the source language (SL) which is aided by extra-linguistic or encyclopaedic knowledge (K). The circle is underneath the others because the source language message initiates the whole interpreting act. The message moves in the direction of the horizontal arrow.
R (TL + K) represents reconstruction (R) in the target language (TL), which is also informed by extra-linguistic or encyclopaedic knowledge (K). The circle overlays the source language circle because the target language message must follow from the source language message.
A (D+CC) represents the analysis (A) which the interpreter uses in both comprehension of the-message and reconstruction of the message. The analysis has two main components, discourse analysis (D) and cross-cultural understanding (CC). The circle overlaps the other two circles because A (D+CC) applies to both the other circles, as is indicated by the downward arrows.
S+ P represents the skills and techniques (S) which an interpreter uses in a professional way and to a professional standard (P) when interpreting. The triangle is superimposed on all circles because the special skills of an interpreter, and the professional standards required apply to the whole process, and differentiate what is achieved in interpreting from other types of bi-lingual communication. → the arrow points away from the original message and its reconstruction to the goal, the act of interpreting.
I stands for Interpreting, the successful communicative act which is dependent on all before the arrow.

preting teachers, so it is fairly natural that their conference interpretings tudies derive from conference interpreting training. Their curriculum designs and textbooks, in turn, offer several major refinements or revisions of conference interpreting processing models.

The first of these is Zhong Weihe's (2003) Knowledge Requirements Formula for Interpreters. Professor Zhong, currently the president of Guangdong University of Foreign Studies and a professor of translation studies, defined interpreting as "a scientific skill as well as an art" (仲伟合, 2003). In his 2001 *review of Gile's Efforts Model and the XiaDa Model*, he listed the skills student interpreters need to master. For consecutive interpreting, those skills included short-term memory, note-taking, note-reading, principles of CI understanding, analysis of speech type, identification of main idea, reconstruction, interpreting figures, coping tactics, preparation, public speaking skills, cross-cultural communication, and professional standards; simultaneous interpreting skills, on the other hand, included cultivating split attention, shadowing exercises, note-taking, listening comprehension, reformulation, simplification, generalization, omission, summarizing, explanation, anticipation, *preparation*, *on-sight interpreting*, handling mistakes, intonation, pronunciation, stress and pauses, interpreting figures/numbers, relay, team work skills, and use of SI facilities (仲伟合, 2001). In 2003, Zhong probed further into Gile's comprehension equation and Lin's interpreting formula, and put forward a Knowledge Requirements Formula for Interpreters (仲伟合, 2003):

$$KI = KL + EK + S(P + AP)$$

According to Zhong, "In this formula, KI = Knowledge Required for an Interpreter, KL = Knowledge for languages, EK = Encyclopedic Knowledge, S (P + AP) = Professional Interpreting Skills and Artistic Presentation Skills" (仲伟合, 2001).

On the basis of this formula, Zhong (2003) proposed that, "interpreting related courses should be designed according to this Knowledge Requirements Formula for Interpreters, i. e. the syllabus should include courses on the improvement of language proficiency and language skills, courses or seminars on encyclopedic knowledge and courses on interpreting skills and professional standards."

A second major contribution was made by Roderick Jones an experienced conference interpreter and conference interpreting trainer at SCIC. In his book *Conference Interpreting Explained* (Jones, 2008)❶, Jones presenteda practical guide to conference interpreting aimed at interpreting students, teachers, colleagues and the public at large, covering such topics as conference interpreting, consecutive interpreting, note-taking, simultaneous interpreting, and the pleasure of interpreting.

The body of the book detailed the specific principles, skills and techniques of both consecutive and simultaneous interpreting. According to Jones, "the three basic stages of a consecutive interpreter's work are understanding, analysis and re-expressing, where 'understanding' refers 'not [to] words but ideas, for it is ideas that have to be interpreted'" (Jones, 2008: 11), in line with Seleskovitch's explana-

---

❶ The first edition of this book was published by St Jerome Publishing in 1998. The second edition was published in 2002. In 2008, Shanghai Foreign Language Education Press published its second edition in China.

tion. In terms of analysis, Jones mentioned analysis of speech types, identification of main ideas, analysis of links, and memory (Jones, 2008: 14-33).

Jones covered practical points for note-taking, including of what to take note, how to do so, abbreviations and symbols, the language in which to make notes, when to take notes, and how to read back notes. He cautioned that "notes are no more than an aid to enhance the work done on the basis of these three key components (understanding, analysis and re-expression). They are not an end in themselves, but a means to an end" (Jones, 2008: 39).

Jones also discussed techniques for simultaneous interpreting, such as when to start speaking, reformulation, the "salami" technique, simplification, generalization, omission, summarizing and recapitulation, explanation, and anticipation, among others (Jones, 2008: 72-123). He noted that "interpretation is not a solipsistic translation exercise, but a practical job of communication", and suggested that it was "probably useful to identify a common thread running through them (techniques) all":

"The first main thread is thus that the simultaneous interpreter must be prepared to diverge in form, and sometimes in literal content, from the letter of the original, in order to achieve the objectives of a good simultaneous interpretation. A second common element is that the interpreter has to adapt not just to their speaker but also to the general context of the meeting and to their audience. In other words, interpretation must be audience-specific and situation-specific." (Jones, 2008: 125)

These refinements shed light on interpreter training and, intentionally or not, reflect the major components of the processing models. This is crucial for any subsequent discussion evaluating and reconstructing the processing model of conference interpreting.

2.4 Summary

This chapter proposes a working definition for conference interpreting, which will be the premise of the study in the following chapters. While interpreting has a long history, modern interpreting can be traced back to the Paris Peace Conference in 1919. Interpreting is different from translation in terms of its origin, processes and language features; as such, the study of interpreting differs from that of translation. Conference interpreting research should emphasize this difference, as a conference interpreter's major task is to facilitate communication by rendering the speaker's message, not the speaker's words. Conference interpreting, while overlapping with other types of interpreting, was the first to establish its status as a profession.

CIR has long been an independent discipline in the West, with more than fifty years of history, but has been seen as a distinct research area in China for just over two decades. However, the models for conference interpreting have not been updated in the past decade. In the future, the conference interpreting market may stagnate, or even shrink, and migration from CIR toward research into other forms of interpreting may occur (Gile, 2006). Researching conference interpreting, and evaluating previous models thereof so as to construct a new one, will be useful for the study of other forms of interpreting, and will better enable researchers to follow possible trends in interpreting research.

A processing model is a research-based representation of conference interpreting that can, at least to some degree, reflect the reality of interpreting. The current prevailing processing models, as cited in this chapter, all developed from Seleskovitch's Interpretive Theory, a meta theory that forms the theoretical foundation of this study, and which will be introduced in the next chapter.

Chapter Three

The Interpretive Theory

3.1 Introduction

Interpretive Theory (IT), also known as the "Theory of Sense", is based on observations of conference interpreting practice, and has been "subsequently extended to the written translation of non-literary or 'pragmatic' texts and to the teaching of translation and interpreting" (Baker, 2004: 112). IT, a major breakthrough in interpreting research was initiated by Danica Seleskovitch, who, along with Marianne Lederer, is a major scholar of the Paris School, one of the most influential schools in interpreting research.

3.1.1 Origin

As discussed in the previous chapter, CIR began in the West in the 1950s. During its Pre-research Period (from the 1950s to the 1960s), CIR focused on the individual experiences of interpreters, and lacked theoretical foundation, while from the 1960s to the early 1970s, CIR's experimental psychology period, its researchers were mainly cognitive psychologists and psycholinguists. Since researchers in this period were not interpreters themselves, there are doubts as to extent to which the CIR conducted in this period helped people to better understand the interpreting process.

Against this research background, IT emerged, in the late 1960s, in France, a country with certain historical and geographical advantages and a language affinity between its language and other European languages. Paris' ESIT was the birthplace of IT, and ESIT scholars are generally referred to as members of the Paris School. Danica Seleskovitch (1921—2001) was the leading scholar of the Paris School, and the initiator of IT. She was an exceptional conference interpreter, a charismatic interpreting teacher, a productive researcher and one of the founders of the AIIC, where she helped to organizeand define the then-budding profession's conditions of exercise. After working as a conference interpreter for many years, she published, in 1968, the first edition of *Interpreting for International Conference*: *Problems of Language and Communication*, a book considered to be the foundation of IT. Subsequently, the Paris School became the research center of CIR's Practitioners Period. The Paris School contends that interpreting is communication within a certain context, and that what should be interpreted is the "sense" or "meaning" of the speaker's message, not its language symbols (e. g., words and sentence structure).

3.1.2 Development and Achievements

IT first began as an interpreting theory, and was later expanded and applied to translation studies. To be specific, Seleskovitch focused her IT research on conference interpreting, while Lederer eventually shifted to the study of written (especially non-literary) translation. The development of IT has gone through three periods. The Beginning Period (mainly the 1970s), followed by the 1968 publication of Seleskovitch's *Interpreting for International Conference: Problems of Language and Communication*, which laid the foundation for IT. The Founding Period refers to the 1980s, during which time the scale and depth of IT developed rapidly. Seleskovitch and Lederer jointly published *Interpréter pour Traduire*, in which they discussed the specific processes and mechanisms of interpreting, with reference to achievements in linguistics and psychology; a comprehensive and profoundly theoretical study of interpreting, the book established IT as a complete theory in translation studies. Finally, the Refining Period, marked by the 1994 publication of Lederer's *La Traduction Aujourd'hui: Le Modèle Interprétatif* (translated into English by Ninon Larché in 2003 and into Chinese by Liu Heping in 2001), which systematically and comprehensively explained and perfected IT.

IT marks a sea change in the history of interpreting studies, as it deviates from Anglo-American analytic philosophy and is underpinned by embodied philosophy. Seleskovitch and Lederer, who were enlightened and inspired by psychology and cognitive science, pioneered study of the psychological process of interpreting, now a popular subject in modern interpreting research.

The development of IT has come in steps, beginning with Seleskovitch's 1968 book, *Interpreting for International Conference: Problems of Language and Communication*, a comprehensive study of interpreting with regard to achievements of linguistics and cognitive science. By defining the nature and tasks of interpreting, Seleskovitch analyzed the difference between interpreting and oral language, the steps of the interpreting process (e. g., listening, comprehension, analysis, memory and expression), and such related issues as extra-linguistic knowledge, linguistic knowledge, cognitive ability, interpreter competence, consecutive and simultaneous interpreting practice, interpreter working conditions, working language, interpreter's workload, causes of interpreter fatigue, etc. The book thus laid the foundation for IT, marked the founding of the Paris School, and made ESIT the research center for IT.

In 1973, Seleskovitch finished her doctoral dissertation (published, in 1975, as *Langage, Langues et Mémoire: Etude de la Prise de Notes en Interprétation Consécutive*), which discussed the importance of note-taking for comprehension and expression in consecutive interpreting, introduced systematic note-taking methods, and analyzed the relationships between notes and comprehension, memory and expression. The book was the theoretical foundation of both IT and the ESIT interpreter training model, and provided a research model for interpreting studies. Based on a corpus, the book was the first ever example of empirical research into interpreting studies, and an example of true scientific research—an approach Seleskovitch asserted should be taken by all future interpreting studies.

In 1978, Lederer finished her doctoral dissertation (published as *La Traduction Simultanée—Expérience et Théorie* in 1981), the first ever study of simultaneous interpreting. By analyzing recordings of professional interpreters, Lederer studied the features of simultaneous interpreting and put forward the "unit of sense" (unité de sens) in interpreting, a key IT notion. She also pointed out that the process of simultaneous interpreting is one in which the interpreter understands and expresses the unit of meaning of the source language continuously (Lederer, 1981).

The formal establishment of IT came in 1984, with the publication of Seleskovitch and Lederer's *Interpréter pour Traduire* (translated into Chinese by Sun Huishuang in 1992). In this collection of papers, the authors analyzed and described the three stages of translation—understanding, memory and expression—from the multiple perspectives of modern linguistics, logic, psychology and communications, repeatedly emphasizing that professional translators and interpreters translate and interpret communicative meanings, not words. In addition, they introduced principles and methods used in teaching interpreting at ESIT, and shared their experiences of preparing for technical interpreting.

In 1989, Seleskovitch and Lederer published *Pédagogie Raisonnée de l'Interprétation*, which focused on interpreting pedagogy for many types of interpreting, including consecutive, simultaneous, relay and video-conference simultaneous interpreting, among others. It was the culmination of ESIT's thirty-year interpreting teaching experience, and marked the formation of its Interpreter Training Model.

In 1994, Lederer published the landmark IT book, *La Traduction Aujourd'hui: Le Modèle Interprétatif* (*Translation Today: The Interpretive Model*), which asserts that good translators usually follow a common translation process, and that analysis of meaning and re-expression are issues common to all translations. The book includes an IT glossary, and is said to mark the perfection of Interpretive Theory.

These above string of achievements are considered the milestones of IT development, and make three key assertions that have contributed to interpreting studies:

1. There are three levels of interpreting-lexical, sentence and discourse. The lexical level is merely word-for-word correspondence, while the sentence level involves interpreting between sentences without regard for contextual setting. IT describes the first and second levels as linguistic interpreting (traduction linguistique) or transcoding (transcodage). The discourse level, however, involves sense equivalence, i.e., interpreting the real sense of the speaker's message, and is the essence of interpretive interpreting.

2. Sense is the true target of interpreting. Before IT, scholars saw interpreting as the conversion of language symbols (i.e., words and structures). IT, however, holds that interpreting is an act of communication, not a result, and is bound within a certain context. What people communicate is meaning—language is merely a carrier of meaning and information. There is thus a clear distinction between word-for-word correspondence and sense equivalence, in that the former is restricted to the interpreting of numbers, titles and proper words, while the latter constructs equivalence between the sense of a discourse in the source language and the sense of that same discourse in the target language. As IT holds that real interpreting is sense equivalence at the discourse level, and that its target is the sense of the whole discourse rather than the semantic sense or the linguistic structures, sense equivalence is thus a fundamental criterion for interpreting.

3. IT consists of three core concepts: deverbalization, the triangular model, and the interpreter training model. Deverbalization, a concept unique to IT, is a process by which the interpreter gleans the speaker's meaning from the linguistic form of the source language, keeps that meaning "deverbalized", and then re-expresses it in the target language. These three concepts will be detailed in the next section.

3.2 Key Concepts

In traditional linguistic translation theories, the translation process consists of only two stages: comprehension and expression. IT holds that interpreting is an act of communication, that the target of interpreting is meaning, not language, and that understanding meaning relies on the interpreter's cognitive complement. Thus, the interpreting process consists of three stages: comprehension/interpretation, deverbalization, and reformulation. The deverbalization stage is considered a breakthrough in translation studies.

3.2.1 Deverbalization

According to Seleskovitch, once meaning is comprehended, it stays without language; the "immediate and deliberate discarding of the wording and retention of the mental representation of the message (concepts, ideas, etc.)" (Seleskovitch, 1978: 9) is called deverbalization, and has two bases: reality, and psychology.

In reality, it is quite common that, after attending a meeting, people cannot remember the exact words and sentences spoken, but can recall and retell clearly the major points they conveyed. According to Seleskovitch, this is because people comprehend and memorize content without memorizing linguistic structure. This phenomenon shows that oral speech is evanescent, as its sounds disappear instantly. However, although the words themselves disappear with the sounds, the graphic signs endure, and the sense of the spoken message remains. Based on the observation and analysis of professional conference interpreters, Seleskovitch found that, after listening to a source text, an interpreter could not repeat the exact words thereof, but could memorize the meaning and interpret the whole text. What an interpreter actually memorizes is not the words s/he has heard, but the utterance she/he intends to say.

From a psychology perspective, human memory can be divided into short-term memory and long-term memory. The capacity of short-term memory, according to American psychology George Miller (1956), is 7±2; in other words, one's short-term memory can retain about seven words at a time, for about two seconds. This has been confirmed in many experiments and is generally accepted. Interpreting is closely related to short-term memory. According to Jensen (1985), short-term memory can be sub-divided into immediate short-time memory and cognitive short-time memory. Immediate short-time memory deals with the phoneme and is capable of handling seven to eight words at once, which stay in the memory for two to three seconds. Cognitive short-time memory is the basis of semantic memory, which stores the smallest unit of sense, separate from the phoneme. To better illustrate the relationship between language, meaning and memory, Seleskovitch divided human memory into substantive memory and verbatim memory, claiming that, in the interpreting process, substantive memory plays a major role, whereas verbatim memory is seldom used.

In the IT interpreting process, the source language is kept in the short-term memory for seconds, at which point "cognitive complements" (Seleskovitch and Lederer, 1989: 247) are activated and transform the source language into sense units. When formed, these sense units immediately meld into larger, deverbalized meaning units. In the interpreting process, deverbalization is a stage between comprehension and reformulation, in which the interpreter gets the cognitive and emotional sense of the source text from the language, and separates sense from, and goes beyond, the language used to convey it. Seleskovitch explained deverbalization by noting that interpretation "is not a direct conversion of the linguistic meaning of the source language to the target language but a conversion from source language to sense, the intermediate link being nonverbal thought which, once consciously grasped, can then be expressed in any language regardless of the words used in the original language" (Seleskovitch, 1977: 28). Liu Heping, a former student of Seleskovitch, explaineddeverbalizaion as "a cognitive process which is known as the data of sensory organ that is transferred into non-sensory knowledge, and we refer it as cognitive memory which, no matter how transient it is, belongs to knowledge acquisition" (刘和平, 2001: 4, 63).

Deverbalization arouses a philosophical issue regarding the relationship between language and thought. People are able to manipulate, develop and state their thoughts through language; however, this does not mean that language equals thought. It is through mutual communication between language and thought that mental impulses (thoughts) are transformed into language, and vice versa. Thoughts do not have any language forms before they are formulated, as knowledge and experienceare not stored in the human brain alongside their language form. The mutual communication between language and thought is the unique feature of human brain.

Deverbalization is a major breakthrough in the history of interpreting studies, one that tries to explain and describe the mental processes of conference interpreters, and is a key stage of the Interpretive Theory's triangular model.

3.2.2 The Triangular Model

Since the 1960s, researchers have put forward various models of interpreting, ranging "from the broader levels of social context to the intricacies of cognitive processes" (Pöchhacker, 2004, 84). There are currently three types of interpreting models: socio-professional and institutional models; interaction models; and information processing/IP models. IP models can be further subdivided into the following: translational process models, multiple tasks models and complex operations models. IT's Triangular Model, one of the earliest IP models, is a translational process model (Pöchhacker, 2004: 95-106).

The first ever description of the interpreting process was provided by a conference interpreter, Jean Herbert, in his book, *Le Manuel de l'Interprete* (*The Interpreter's Handbook: How to Become a Conference Interpreter*). In the book, Herbert explained the interpreting process as one of comprehension, transformation and expression (Herbert, 1952: 9). Building on that, Seleskovitch (1962) claimed that an interpreter goes through three stages in the interpreting process: comprehension, separation of sense and language, and re-expression. This process is not a transformation of language symbols, or a search for equivalent expressions in the target language, but rather a process of understanding and re-expressing the sense of the received message. Seleskovitch (1968: 8) further explained the interpreting process by noting that the process of consecutive and simultaneous interpreting can be divided into three steps: "first, auditory perception of a linguistic utterance which carries meaning, apprehension of the language and comprehension of the message through a process of analysis and exegesis; second, immediate and deliberate discarding of the wording and retention of the mental representation of the message; third, production of a new utterance in the target language which must meet a dual requirement: it must express the original message in its entirety, and it must be geared to the recipient production" (Seleskovitch, 1978: 8). In other words, the process is one of perception/listening, followed by comprehension/understanding, and then by expression, and is thus "a triangular process not a linear process of transfer" (Seleskovitch, 1978: 37, 85). The better the interpreter understands the speaker, the easier it is for the former to express the latter's opinion in the former's own words. It is difficult for the interpreter to notice the comprehension stage that lies between listening and expression; the comprehension process is an earlier form of deverbalization.

Sense is the target of interpreting in IT. In his book, *What Is Literature*, famous French philosopher, playwright and novelist Jean Paul Sartrepointed out that sense "never exists in words, but it helps to understand the meaning of each word. Although literature works realize themselves through words, they should on no account confine themselves to words. Sometimes it happens that one reads a literary work word by word, but he/she doesn't understand the sense of the work" (Sartre, 1988: 50 – 51). According to Lederer (2002), sense forms when linguistic knowledge and extra-linguistic knowledge are merged.

Selekovitch also clarified the concept of sense, noting that it is "conscious", "made up of the linguistic meaning aroused by speech sounds and of a cognitive addition to it", "nonverbal, and is separated with the linguistic form in human's cognitive memory" (Selekovitch, 1978: 336). This clarification laid the foundation for IT by depicting interpreting as a process of comprehending and expressing the sense of the message, based on the interpreter's knowledge. Accordingly, Selekovitch (1977: 27 – 23) redefined the three stages of the interpreting process as comprehension/interpretation, deverbalizaton and reformulation. In 1984, Selekovitch and Lederer formalized the structure of the triangular model of interpretation, in their book, *Interpréter pour Traduire* (Selekovitch & Lederer, 1984: 168, 185) (see Figure 3.1).

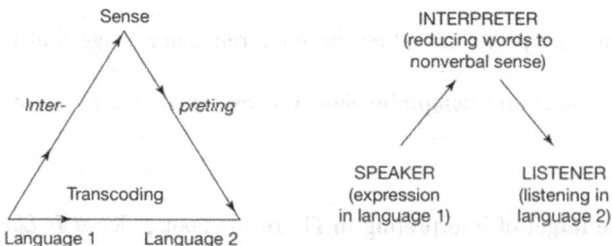

Figure 3. 1 Seleskovitch's Triangular Model (two versions)

(**from Seleskovitch and Lederer, 1984: 185, 168**)

The triangular model shows: interpreting is a process that starts from Language 1 (comprehension), goes to Sense (vouloirdire, i.e., what was meant to be said), and then to Language 2 (reformulation). Language 1 and Language 2 form the bottom vertices of the triangle, while Sense is at its peak. The base line of the triangle refers to the transcoding process, in which Language 1 is directly transformed into Language 2; the interpreting process (the interpretive translation process) goes from Language 1 to Sense and then to Language 2, and is thus completely different from transcoding process.

This triangular model is based on tree hypotheses; namely, that interpreting is a psychological process; that the target of interpreting is the sense and emotions conveyed by the source language, not the language that carries them; and that language and thought remain separate, such that language symbols are not involved in understanding and storing meaning.

The triangular model is the earliest information processing (IP) model in interpreting studies, and sheds light on many subsequent interpreting models, including the SI processing model by Moser-Mercer (1978: 151–152; 2002: 152–153), Lederer's eight-mental-operation model for SI (Lederer, 1981: 50), Stenzl's communicative information flow model (Stenzl, 1983: 45), the socio-linguistically-sensitive process model by Cokely (1992: 124), the SI processing model by Setton (1999: 65) and Chernov's probability prediction model (Chernov, 2004: 91–106). In all of these models, extra-linguistic knowledge and knowledge about theme or context are all the key components in the information processing process (Cokely's model also involves cultural awareness). The models also share the cognitive complements opinion with Seleskovitch's triangular model.

Since Seleskovitch had already put identified the three stages of the interpreting process in 1962, and since the Paris School and IT dominated interpreting studies in the 1970s to 1980s, it is reasonable to conclude that these subsequent interpreting models derived from the cognitive psychological perspective of Seleskovitch's triangular model.

3.2.3 The Interpreter Training Model

The Paris School, chiefly known for IT, is a school of interpreting studies that originated in France in the 1960s and 1970s. Scholars from the Paris School have focused on two aspects of interpreting studies: the cognitive process of interpreting, and the study of conference interpreting pedagogy, also known as the ESIT model. Dating from the 1980s, the ESIT model is a series of principles and methods of conference interpreting teaching.

According to Gile (1995), conference interpreting includes both simultaneous and consecutive interpreting. After the First World War, there was increased demand for interpreting. In 1930, the first interpreter training school was established, in Mannheim, Germany, and in the 1940s many other translation schools or departments were established in universities across the globe, including at the University of Geneva in Switzerland, the University of Vienna in Austria, and Georgetown University in the US. In 1957, ESIT was founded in France, and in 1969, MIIS (Monterey Institute of International Studies) was founded in the U.S., beginning a new era of large-scale, professional conference interpreter training in Europe and America.

Chapter Three The Interpretive Theory

Although conference interpreting training is booming in Europe and North America, many interpreting schools do not fully understand the essence and principles of professional conference interpreter training, and their training programs are guided by the comparative linguistic perspective of translation; according to Seleskovitch, they "consider translation as merely a linguistic activity and translation teaching is merely language teaching" (Seleskovitch and Lederer, 1984: 177). Seleskovitch criticized this perspective and refused to teach interpreting from the linguistic perspective of translation, arguing that interpreting is an activity in which information is exchanged, and that its target is sense; as such, the primary goal of interpreting training and practice must be the comprehension and expression of sense (Seleskovitch, 1978: 333-341).

Therefore, according to Jean Delisle (1988), a scholar of the Paris School, a distinction should be made between "pedagogical or academic translation—translation as a teaching tool" and the "pedagogy of translation—the teaching of translation proper"; the former centers on the teaching of foreign languages through bilingual comparative translation exercises in traditional language classes, while the latter trains a person who has already mastered a foreign language to become a professional interpreter. These two types of translation correspond with Lederer's (2003: 134-139, 152) concepts of "linguistic translation" and "interpretive translation."

Distinguishing between pedagogical translation and pedagogy of translation differentiates between the interpreting teaching offered at a translation school or department, and that available from a general interpreting class at a foreign language school. This differentiation contributes greatly to the global professionalization and standardization of conference interpreter training, and the development of an effective model for the training of conference interpreters (Seleskovitch and Lederer, 1989).

Seleskovitch taught at ESIT from 1957 until her retirement in 1990. From 1959 to 1963, she also served as the executive secretary of the AIIC, and made the ESIT model for interpreter training AIIC practice; the AIIC also recommends that interpreting training institutes in Europe adopt the following ESIT model principles and methods:

1) Candidates for conference interpreting programs must first receive a bachelor's degree;

2) To ensure quality of education, candidates must pass a strict entrance examination, as well as interpreting skills tests at mid-term and graduation. A candidate who fails these tests is not qualified to be a conference interpreter and will not receive a degree;

3) Interpreting teachers must be interpreters themselves; scholars or language teachers without interpreting experience are not qualified to be interpreting teachers;

4) *Interpreting training is not foreign language teaching*, and teachers teach interpreting skills only, not language. Students must have a good command of the working languages before beginning to learn interpreting skills;

5) Students majoring in conference interpreting must learn both consecutive and simultaneous interpreting;

6) To ensure interpreting quality, the interpreter should not do simultaneous

interpreting into language B, and students will only receive training for single direction simultaneous interpreting into language A;❶ and,

7) Conference interpreting programs's yllabus, curriculum and language pairs should reflect the real needs in the interpreting market (Seleskobitch and Lederer, 1984: 172, 1989; 闫素伟、邵炜, 2011).

These aspects were later adopted by the AIIC's training committee, which recommended, on the basis of 3), that conference interpreting program course leadersshould be world-renowned professional interpreters or AIIC members. To ensure its leading position in the field of interpreting, the AIIC added four interpreter training principles to the previous seven:

8) All course instructors should be native speakers of the language pairs involved in the course;

9) The syllabus should include the code of professional ethics;

10) Teachers should recommend their graduate students apply for membership in international interpreter organizations (for example, the AIIC), and students who fail the graduation exam should not be encouraged to work as interpreters; and,

11) Interpreting training institutes should remain in contact with international

---

❶ Language A refers to the interpreter's native language; language B refers to a non-native language of which the interpreter has a good command, and can use as the target language of consecutive and simultaneous interpreting; language C refers to a language the interpreter can fully understand and interpret into language A or B, but cannot use it as the target language. In the United Nations, having a good command of Asian and Arabian languages is too difficult for many Western interpreters, and this constraint on simultaneous interpreting into language B has been abolished. Interpreters from China and Arabic countries must conduct bidirectional simultaneous interpreting.

interpreting services (for example, the AIIC), and invite those services' chief interpreters and representatives to serve as examiners for graduation exams. They should also recommend their graduates to the clients (AIIC, 2010).

Nos. 1) to 7) are often referred to, by the international interpreting community, as the ESIT model, while Nos. 1) to 11) are referred to as the AIIC School Policy. Both have been applied by many interpreting training institutes.

Moreover, in their book, *Pédagogie Raisonnée de l'Interprétation*, Seleskovitch and Lederer (1989) put forward additional specific training principles:

1) Students should first have a good command of consecutive interpreting skills before starting to learn simultaneous interpreting (1989: 102-103);

2) For most of their time in interpreting training, students should listen to the speaker speaking in his/her native language (1989: 51); and,

3) Any information that cannot be noted using non-linguistic symbols should be noted in the target language, rather than the source language (1989: 37).

In recent decades, there have been some changes made to the ESIT model, triggered by variations in the interpreting market; for example, a language enhancement program has been added to the syllabus to enhance students' language ability. This shows that the ESIT model is an open, practical and developing system that keeps pace with the times and changing client needs. As a result, it is no longer just the standard for interpreting training among European countries, but also an applicable training model for China and Arabic countries, where languages are quite distinct from European languages.

3.3 IT and Processing Models of Conference Interpreting

IT was the dominant interpreting theory in the 1970s and 1980s and, more important, is one of the earliest well-established theories in CIR. More recently, however, other interpreting theories and models have arisen at different levels that are based on IT and either adopt the basic concepts of IT or refine them to some degree.

IT's focus on sense, rather than language, as the target of interpreting has become the presupposition of conference interpreting processing models, and its three-stage process (comprehension, deverbalization and re-expression) is reflected in emergent interpreting models at various levels. In large part, this is because most scholars of the Paris School are interpreters themselves, and IT reflects their real-life interpreting practice and experience, while the Paris School's ESIT training model sheds light on the nature of the interpreting process.

To sum up, since the introduction and wide-spread acceptance of IT, various interpreting models and theories have emerged that accept its concepts and are built on refining or retorting it. Among these, processing models for conference interpretingneed to be evaluated and reconstructed; IT is an applicable theoretical foundation for such an evaluation and reconstruction.

3.4 Summary

In this chapter, the author introduces the origin, development and achievements of IT, which was first advanced by ESIT scholars Danica Seleskovitch and Marianne

Lederer in the 1970s. Since then, Seleskovitch and Lederer have published numerous books and supervised a significant number of dissertations and theses that have helped IT retain its influence to this day. IT is the chief theory of the Paris School, and has undergone three developmental periods since its creation—the Beginning Period, the Founding Period and the Refining Period. IT regards sense, rather than language, to be the target of interpreting, and holds that interpreting can be divided into three level-lexical, sentence, and discourse—the third of which is considered real interpreting under IT, as the "sense" targeted by IT is the sense of the whole discourse. Based on that understanding, IT includes the following key concepts: deverbalization, the triangular model and the interpreter training model.

Among the various types of interpreting, conference interpreting is the most demanding. Processing models of conference interpreting share IT's understanding of "sense" as the interpreting target. The next chapter will evaluate previous processing models of conference interpreting to identify space for reconstruction. This evaluation is inevitably conducted within the scope of the theoretical foundation laid in this chapter.

Chapter Four

Evaluation of Processing Models of Conference Interpreting

4.1 Correlations

Pöchhacker (2004) asserted that there are different levels of modeling in interpreting studies, including Seleskovitch's Triangular Model and Gile's Effort Models. Gile (1995), in an examination of simultaneous interpreting based on Seleskovitch's three-stage interpreting process (comprehension, deverbalization, re-expression), specified the basic efforts in the interpreting process (L, P, M, C) and emphasized the importance of comprehension, by putting forward his comprehension formula.

However, Pöchhacker's research mainly covers CIR in the West, and research findings from CIR in China are not included in his study. Over the past decade, numerous fruitful research initiatives have been pursued by Chinese scholars, the XiaDa Model (1999) being an example thereof; the prevailing processing model in

China, the XiaDa Model extends Gile's formula by adding skills and professional standards. Another example is Zhong's (2003) Knowledge Requirements Formula for Interpreters, which is based on Gile's comprehension formula and the XiaDa Model. Finally, Roderick Jones' book, *Conference Interpreting Explained*, first published in 2002, bears many similarities to the ESIT training model.

Taken chronologically, these models represent different periods in the development of CIR. Gile's Effort Models were proposed in 1995, between CIR's Practitioners and Renewal Periods, a time when CIR in the West was beginning to take wing and become interdisciplinary. Gile took a different approach, shifting the focus from the interpreting process to the interpreter himself; Gile's Effort Models mark the beginning of CIR within the context of globalization.

The XiaDa Model was proposed in 1999, two decades after the implementation of China's reform and opening-up policy. Two years after the XiaDa Model was proposed, China joined the World Trade Organization. At that time, southeast China was developing extremely rapidly, and there had been a sudden boom in the interpreting market. Interpreting became a growing profession in China, one which badly required *rules and regulations* so as to develop in the right direction. For that reason, the XiaDa Model emphasizes skills and professional standards.

Roderick Jones' *Conference Interpreting Explained* was first published in 2002, a time Gile (1994) called the "Renaissance" of CIR in the West, and during which many research centers and interpreter training institutions were founded around the world. Jones' book is the first detailed explanation of conference interpreter training,

Chapter Four Evaluation of Processing Models of Conference Interpreting

and gives samples and explanations of the skills to be taught in various interpreter training programs around the world.

Zhong's Knowledge Requirements Formula for Interpreters was put forward in 2003, four years after the XiaDa Model was proposed. Zhong is a professor at Guangdong University of Foreign Studies, in Guangdong Province, the first province in which China's 1978 reform and opening-up policy was implemented. Interpreting is in great demand in Guangdong, as is interpreter training. Since the XiaDa Model already incorporates components of interpreting, Zhong took a different approach and expanded it into a human activity in which the interpreter's knowledge is the research objective.

Correlations exist between the aforementioned processing models and their refinements. In the global context, expanded research approaches, changes in market demand and the development and regulation of a profession stimulated the development of models.

As mentioned previously, IT holds that sense is the target of interpreting, and that the interpreting process comprises three stages—comprehension, deverbalization, and re-expression. Conference interpreting, whether consecutive or simultaneous, involves the comprehension and re-expression of the speaker's deverbalized sense. However, such a division of the interpreting process is too general, as there are a variety of skills required at different stages of the process. Given that processing models of conference interpreting have adopted the concepts of IT, they also share some basic components of IT's interpreting process, a detailed evaluation of which will be conducted in this section, with specific regard to comprehension, analysis, working memory and re-expression.

4.2 Comprehension

Conference interpreting began in the West, mainly in Europe, where most languages belong to the Indo-European language family (Fernand Mossé, 1990: 3), giving rise to similarities that facilitate comprehension of the continent's various languages, and permitting effective interpreting through only two phases: comprehension and re-expression.

However, as a result of globalization, exchanges among countries have begun to increase and more and more trade zones have been established in different regions around the world. As such, there is a growing demand for interpreting between European languages and (for example) Asian orArabic languages. There exist huge differences in pronunciation, grammar, lexicon, semantics and pragmatics between these two groups of languages, making comprehension between Western and Asian/Arabic languages very different from that among European languages. This has occasioned a drastic change in CIR.

Daniel Gile was the first scholar to notice this shift, and to emphasize comprehension as an interpreting requirement. A conference interpreter and member of the AIIC, Gile holds a PhD in Japanese, and his research into conference interpreting is based on interpreting between European and Asian languages. His comprehension equation (C = KL + EKL + A; i.e., Comprehension = Knowledge for the Language

Chapter Four Evaluation of Processing Models of Conference Interpreting

+ Extra-linguistic Knowledge + Analysis) emphasizes the pivotal role of comprehension in the interpreting process, as the interface between analysis andknowledge (both of the language and extra-linguistic).

However, Gile's equation is still too general, and fails to make some points clear. First, it does not emphasize that interpreting is a communicative activity that is different from translation, and that comprehension in the interpreting process therefore requires different language skills than does comprehension in the translation process. As such, it does not identify the specific skill(s) the interpreter should emphasize to achieve better comprehension. Second, it does not specify what kind of analysis is taking place in the interpreting process.

Lin holds that "comprehension alone is not enough to enable interpretation" (林郁如, 1999: xxi), and researchers of the XiaDa Model have extended Gile's formula and reformulated the interpreting process as:

$$S + C \{L + K + A\} + P \rightarrow I$$

The formula asserts that the interpreter's skills and techniques (S) are applied to comprehension (C) in a professional manner (P) to produce a successful act of interpreting (I). Comprehension (C) is informed by language knowledge (L), extra-linguistic knowledge (K), and an analysis of the whole situation (A)(林郁如, 1999: xxiii).

The XiaDa Model expands language (L) to include source language (SL) and target language (TL); comprehension (C) in the XiaDa Model is comprehension of the source language, aided by extra-linguistic or encyclopedic knowledge (i.e. C

(SL+K)). The XiaDa Model is very macro, although it specifies that source language is what the interpreter comprehends. By using merely a plus sign "+" to link elements, it fails to present the relationship between SL (source language knowledge), K (knowledge) and A (analysis).

Zhong, in his Knowledge Requirements Formula for Interpreters (See 2.3.3), also refined comprehension in the interpreting process. He reviewed Gile's Effort Models and the XiaDa Model to identify the skills that student interpreters needed to master, generalizing them in his formula as S (P + AP) (i.e. Professional Interpreting Skills and Artistic Presentation Skills). Zhong pointed out that training in these skills alone is not sufficient to produce a qualified interpreter; courses about language, language skills and encyclopedic knowledge should also be included (仲伟合, 2003). In Zhong's formula, knowledge for language (KL), encyclopedic knowledge (EK) and professional interpreting skills (P) drive comprehension, which corresponds with the Effort Models in terms of knowledge, and with the XiaDa Model in terms of skills. Zhong's refinement focuses more on training, which lacks integration of knowledge and skills. The real interpreting process involves not only the *interpreter*, but also speakers and listeners, a much broader range than is currently addressed in the interpreter training process.

Roderick Jones (2008) also mentioned comprehension in his *Conference Interpreting Explained*, referring to "understanding" as being "not of words but ideas, for it is ideas that have to be interpreted". Since his book focuses more on interpreter training, his explanation of "understanding" corresponds with those offered by Seleskovitch and Gile. However, both Zhong's formula and Jones' explanations give rise to a crucial question—how should the interpreter integrate these identified skills and knowledge so as to comprehend the message?

To evaluate comprehension in the aforementioned processing models, this study addresses the following aspects: K (knowledge, including knowledge of the language and extra-linguistic or encyclopedic knowledge), A (analysis), P (professionalism or professional standard) and S (interpreting skills). Having found this common ground, questions concerning comprehension still exist. Since linguistic and cultural differences between East and West are stumbling blocks for comprehension, knowledge, analysis, professionalism and skills are too general references for future conference interpreters, and a more direct representation is needed. Hence, the reconstructing of the processing model will specify comprehension.

4.3 Analysis

To examine the aspect, analysis, it is first necessary to clarify its functionand target. The interpreter conducts different types of analysis at each step of the interpreting process; that is to say, analysis conducted for comprehension is different from that conducted for re-expression. As it is beyond question that the interpreter does not analyze merely for the sake of analysis, analysis must therefore be a necessary step that correlates with other stepsin the interpreting process. Analysis is to the interpreting process, as note-taking is to working memory; just as the interpreter takes notes to facilitate his/her working memory, the interpreter conducts analysis to facilitate the interpreting process.

In Gile's Effort Models, analysis is a major component of his comprehension equation; however, he does not specify the exact type of analysis involved. The XiaDa Model, in contrast, specifies that analysis consists of both discourse analysis and cross-cultural analysis (expressed as A (D + CC)). The interpreter applies analysis in both the comprehension and reconstruction of the message (林郁如, 1999: xxi-xxiv). While the XiaDa Model advances Gile's equation, it does not address whether the interpreter conducts the same analysis (discourse analysis and cross-cultural analysis) for both the comprehension and reconstruction of the message.

Jones (2008), in *Conference Interpreting Explained*, specified analysis as the analysis of speech types and links. Though the study of speech types and links falls within the definition of discourse analysis, Jones' specification is different, as his specification focuses on the oral form of the source material.

Interpreting can be regarded as an act of cross-cultural communication, so the inclusion of cross-cultural analysis in the interpreting process makes sense. The XiaDa Model's reason for including discourse analysis, however, is less clear, and one with which this author does not fully agree.

Discourse analysis is derived from Zellig Harris' (1952) study of structuralism, and originally fell into the scope of linguistic studies. Over the past 60 years, discourse analysis has been applied to many other subjects, including semiotics, psychology, anthropology, sociology, literature and information science. Discourse analysis is not

Chapter Four   Evaluation of Processing Models of Conference Interpreting

recognized as an independent subject, which has caused some controversy over its goals. Some scholars believe that discourse analysis is an interpretive activity, as it aims to help the reader better understand the meaning of a given discourse, or the meaning the author wants to express. Other scholars believe that discourse analysis is an explanatory activity that seeks to explain why a given discourse conveysa certain meaning(s). Still other scholars have tried to shed light on this controversy. Halliday and Hasan pointed out that the linguistic analysis of a discourse is "explanation" rather than "interpretation"; "interpretation" reveals WHAT meaning a discourse conveys, while "explanation" describes HOW it conveys such meaning (Halliday & Hasan, 1976: 327). From this perspective, discourse analysis can be seen as a linguistic explanation of how a given discourse conveys its meaning. Such analysis is normally conducted by linguists in written form; however, no written material can exactly correspond with every word the speaker utters.

Obviously, the interpreter's target when analyzing a discourse is not to linguistically explain how it conveys a meaning, but what meaning it conveys; in other words, it is interpretive, rather than explanatory. Analysis in the interpreting process therefore does not fall into the scope of discourse analysis, and the application of discourse analysis in the interpreting process, as shown in the XiaDa Model, is not appropriate. Therefore, a different specification of analysis is needed to reconstruct the processing model.

4.4 Working Memory

IT expanded the interpreting process by considering deverbalization—what Seleskovitch (1978: 9) called the "immediate and deliberate discarding of the wording and retention of the mental representation of the message (concepts, ideas, etc.)" —in addition to comprehension and re-expression. In comprehension and analysis, the interpreter does discard the speaker's wording; however, conference interpreting involves dealing with massive amounts of information (see section 2.2.1), making it difficult for the interpreter to spare the mental space and energy needed to store the verbalized messages. Thus, memorization is a necessary step for achieving deverbalization in IT.

Human memory can be divided into long-term memory and short-term memory, although the term "working memory" (coined by Baddeley and Hitch (1974)) is generally used in CIR to represent both. In the interpreting process, the interpreter employs both long-term memory and short-term memory to create their working memory. For the interpreter, however, memorization has three shortcomings—the limitations of short-term memory; the inactiveness of information stored in long-term memory; and, the effects of high work pressures on memory.

To improve the interpreter's working memory, it is necessary to step back and review its goal. Like analysis, working memory is a facilitator of the interpreting process. Since the target of interpreting is the deverbalized sense, so too should be the target of working memory; verbatim memory is inapplicable to interpreting.

Short-term memory has already been studied extensively by psychologists and interpreting researchers (see section 2.2.3). Memory training for interpreters focuses more on developing short-term memory, which the interpreter facilitates through analysis and note-taking.

Gile's Efforts Model incorporates Short-term Memory Effort into the equation for simultaneous interpreting and phase I of consecutive interpreting. However, this does not offer a complete picture of memorization, as an interpreter must activate knowledge stored in his/her long-term memory to enable his/her short-term memory to memorize new information. Lin did not incorporate working memory as a component of the XiaDa Model; instead, he included it among the skills the interpreter applies in the interpreting process. Interpreting skills are major components in the XiaDa Model, but working memory is not highlighted among them. In Jones' *Conference Interpreting Explained*, analysis and visualization are proposed as working memory training techniques; the importance of working memory in conference interpreting is that it enables the interpreter to reduce massive information in a concise and simple manner, thus making them easier to remember. Zhong Weihe, in his Knowledge Requirements Formula for Interpreters, proposed that interpreter training courses should include courses on interpreting skills. However, as in the previous models his study refines, working memory in general is not highlighted.

Reviewing these processing models and their refinements reveals a controversy regarding the role of working memory in processing models. Gile and Jones incorporated "memory" in the interpreting process, but did not incorporate long-term memory as a part thereof. The XiaDa Model and Zhong Weihe's formula both include a variety of interpreting skills, working memory being just one of these. Whether or not working memory should be incorporated as an independent component in the interpreting process depends on the function of working memory and its correlation with other components of the processing model.

4.5 Re-expression

Seleskovitch claimed re-expression was the production of a new utterance in the target language that both expresses the original message in its entirety, and is geared to recipient production (Seleskovitch: 1978: 8). In some processing models for conference interpreting, other words are used as substitutions for "re-expression". Gile, for example, refers to Speech Production Effort in his Effort Models, and also incorporates Coordination, claiming that the interpreter has to coordinate the message in order to re-express it. Lin usedthe term "Reconstruction" in the XiaDa Model; since language in this model expands encompasses both the source and target languages, the term refers to reconstruction in the target language/knowledge, based on the interpreter's comprehension of the source language/knowledge and cross-cultural analysis.

Jones did refer to re-expression in his book, explained its role in conference interpreting, and proposed practical tactics for it. Taking a practitioner's approach, Jones' tactics for re-expression have a much wider vision, covering not only interpreting techniques, but also working environment and clients. Zhong emphasized the importance of re-expression and proposed that interpreters develop, not only professional interpreting skills, but also artistic presentation skills, as interpreting is "a scientific skill as well as an art" (仲伟合, 2003).

Whatever terms are used in these models, they convey the need to re-express the speaker's message in the target language. However, re-expression alone is not enough for the interpreter to meet the dual requirement Seleskovitch set forth. More often than not, the interpreter encounters problems with language and knowledge, and the aforementioned processing models put much more emphasis on the steps preceding re-expression; re-expression, as an independent component, is less studied in CIR.

However, in Second Language Acquisition, a sub-discipline of linguistics, oral language development is studied to provide strategies for teachers to improve students' oral language performance and proficiency. Oral language development in Second Language Acquisition resembles re-expression in the interpreting process, for both involve the speaker's ability to express an idea. Oral language enables the speaker to express his/her idea in his/her language, while re-expression refers to the interpreter's ability to convey that idea accurately in a target language. Refinement of re-expression shall focus on the issue of re-expression itself, i. e., strategies that may improve the interpreter's re-expression abilities.

4.6 Summary

In this chapter, the author evaluates processing models for conference interpreting and their refinements, including Daniel Gile's Effort Models, Lin Yuru's XiaDa Model, Roderick Jones' *Conference Interpreting Explained*, and Zhong Weihe's Knowledge Requirements Formula for Interpreters. Taking a chronological approach, the author first discussed the correlations between these process models and their refinements. Given the trend towards globalization, approaches to CIR shift with the changing demands of the interpreting market. With China's boom in interpreting and language service market, CIR in China is gaining more and more reviews and critics in the global CIR community. Conference interpreting in China is a budding profession, which leads to the need to develop new processing models.

The chapter has also provided a detailed evaluation of these processing models, in terms of comprehension, analysis, working memory, and re-expression. The questions posed led to either further specification of these aspects, or expansion of the interpreting process. In the next chapter, the processing model will be reconstructed, with clues drawn from the evaluation in this chapter.

Chapter Five

Reconstruction of the Processing Model of Conference Interpreting

In the previous chapter, four aspects of processing models of conference interpreting are evaluated. Given that the aim of this chapter is to reconstruct the processing model for conference interpreting, these four aspects will be refined or reconstructed, as necessary.

5.1 Active Listening (AL)

The first aspect to be studied is comprehension. First, it is necessary to clarify the goal of comprehension in conference interpreting. IT holds that, since sense is the target of interpreting, it must logically also be the target of comprehension. To be specific, according to Selekovitch, sense is deverbalized—i.e., separated from language—and it is this deverbalized sense that is the target of comprehension in IT. However, this target is too general for a detailed study of comprehension, so this study adopts a linguistic approach to clarify it.

Over the past two decades, Noam Chomsky's Transformational-Generative Grammar (TG Grammar) approach—and especially its Syntactic Description (SD) Theory—has become prevalent in linguistic studies. Scholars of the TG Grammar school have asserted that the deep structure of a sentence determines its meaning, while the surface structure determines its form (Chomsky and Schüützenberger, 1963). This is crucial for the study of meaning in translation studies, and translation research scholars in Europe and in America have had fairly meaningful debates on this issue. Nida (1964) explained the translation process, from a TG Grammar perspective, as starting from the surface structure of the source, moving on to its deep structure, and then to the surface structure of the receptor. Liu Miqing (1985) held that the correspondence between source and target languages lies not in surface structure, but in deep structure. He then diagrammed the process of English-Chinese translation, as shown in Figure 5.1, below:

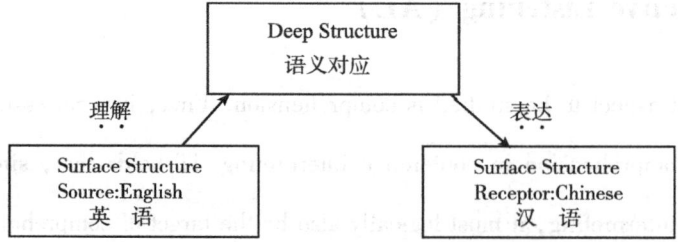

Figure **5.1　The Process of E-C Translation by Liu Miqing** (刘宓庆, 1985: 15)

Based on Chomsky, Nida and Liu, therefore, the targets of comprehension are

Chapter Five Reconstruction of the Processing Model of Conference Interpreting

both the surface and deep structure of the source language. This clarification sets the premise for refining comprehension in IT.

According to the working definition proposed previously (see section 2.2.1), conference interpreting overlaps with other types of interpreting, as conference speakers usually have rather high political, social or academic status that affects the sense of their comments; for example, they might speak as a government leader who is explaining or stating official opinions, or as the representative of a certain field who is illustrating his/her professional understandings, experiences andachievements. Their presentations are usually prepared ahead of the conference, and may be bound by a script, an outline, a series of jotted-down notes or key words, or may entirely impromptu; whatever the form of the speaker's preparation and presentation, however, the interpreter must seize the main idea instantly.

It is without doubt that knowledge of language is the first step towards comprehension, and that, since interpreting is an act of oral communication, oral language skills (listening and speaking) should be emphasized; listening, for example, is obviously a specific skill needed for comprehension. However, the study of listening within the scope of interpreting study differs from the study of listening as it relates to foreign language teaching. In foreign language teaching, the major issues around listening mostly concern the source language itself (i.e., pronunciation, intonation, vocabulary, grammar, oral expressions, slang, idioms, etc.). In interpreting study, listening is concerned with communication, meaning it is not merely a language skill, but also an approach to comprehending the speaker's underlying message.

Processing Model of Conference Interpreting: Evaluation and Reconstruction
会议口译加工模式：评估与重构

A conference interpreter has to comprehend, by listening, both the surface structure and deep structure of a speaker's message. He/she must be able to listen to a message in his/her native language and reproduce that message in a foreign language, and vice versa. Sometimes, listening to one's native language can be a problem, as deep structure is hidden from the interpreter during the listening process; as such listening is completely different for conference interpreting than for language learning.

Active Listening (AL) is a means of getting both the surface and deep structure of a speaker's message, whether in interpreter's native language or a foreign language. AL is derived from Carl Rogers' psychological studies, and was originally labeled "reflection of feelings" (Gordon, 2001: 297). The term was first used by Dr. Thomas Gordon in his book, *Leader Effective Training* (*L. E. T.*), and promoted as a necessary interpersonal communication skill for leaders seeking to help group members resolve their problems (Gordon, 2001). Gordon held that the interpersonal communication process "requires the *expression* of a sender and the *impression* of a receiver, (and) effective or complete communication, then, only occurs when IMPRESSION = EXPRESSION" (Gordon, 2001: 57). Figure 5.2, below, diagrams the interpersonal communication process in *L. E. T.*:

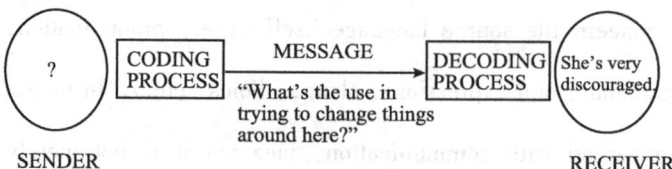

Figure 5.2 Interpersonal Communication Process by Gordon (Gordon, 2001: 57)

Chapter Five Reconstruction of the Processing Model of Conference Interpreting

Gordon explained that "real understanding of another person happens only when the receiver's impression (the results of decoding) matches closely what the sender intended in her expression" (Gordon, 2001: 57). To ensure effective communication, Gordon proposed a series of methods, including door openers, passive listening, acknowledgement responses, active listening, and avoiding "roadblocks to communication" (Gordon, 2001: 53-80). Active listening is about "frequent and continuous feedback of the results of the receiver's decoding" and "is certainly not complex. Listeners need only restate, in their own language, their impression of the expression of the sender. It's a check: is my impression acceptable to the sender?" (Gordon, 2001: 62). In the following diagram (Figure 5.3, below), for example, the sender's message is "What's the use of trying to change things around here?" The receiver decodes this message as, "She is feeling very discouraged." and feeds this decoded version back to the sender:

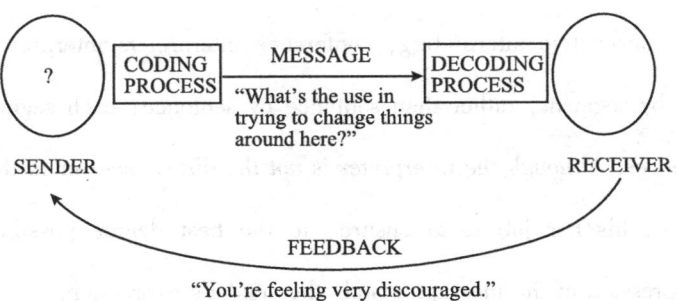

Figure 5.3 Active Listening by Gordon (Gordon, 2001: 61)

Gordon probed further into the concepts providing the underlying rationale for active listening—empathy and acceptance. Empathy is "the capacity to put oneself in the shoes of others and understand their 'personal world of meaning'", while acceptance is "feeling good about what a person is doing" and "(accepting) the other person just as she is at the moment" (Gordon, 2001: 63-65). This rationale is crucial for conference interpreters; the interpreter must first be an expert in communication, as she/he may encounter various speakers, each with a unique way of coding their message (unique ways of expression), and must be able to fully understand all of their messages. AL in communication means fully concentrating on both the verbal and non-verbal message, rather than just hearing the speaker's words.

There are different degrees of AL. The first degree is repeating, which means to repeat the message using *exactly the same* words used by the speaker. The second degree is paraphrasing, which involves rendering the message using words and phrase arrangements *similar* to those used by the speaker. The third degree is reflecting, in which the interpreter renders the message using *his/her own* words and sentence structure. In consecutive interpreting, conference interpreters interpret a speech or talk segment by segment, rather than sentence by sentence; each segment contains *several sentences. Although the interpreter is not the direct receiver in the communication process, his/her job is to ensure, to the best degree possible, that the receiver's impression of the message equals the sender's expression.

AL in conference interpreting requires the interpreter to: 1) listen actively to the speaker's verbal message; 2) receive the speaker's non-verbal message; and, 3) analyze the message's information hierarchy. AL in the interpreting process falls

Chapter Five Reconstruction of the Processing Model of Conference Interpreting

into two dimensions. At the sentence level, paraphrasing is required, and the interpreter should understand the meaning of each sentence. At the discourse level, reflecting occurs, and the interpreter should be able to reflect all the segment's information, both major and minor.

The following examples from Level 2 of CATTI[①] illustrate the two dimensions of AL in the interpreting process. In Part I of the English Language Skills Test of Level 2 of CATTI, candidates listen to short passages and then decide whether corresponding statements about those passages are true or false. This test corresponds with the first dimension of AL-paraphrasing.

Example 1:
AUDIO: "Tens of thousands of youngsters from low-income families who were eligible for a children's health insurance program in Florida, instead of being allowed into the program, were diverted by state officials to a long waiting list." (卢敏, 2009: 70)

STATEMENT: The children's health insurance program in Florida was intended to help kids from low-income families. (True) (卢敏, 2009: 51)

The key to understanding this sentence lies in the phrase "be eligible for". According to Longman's contemporary dictionary, someone who is eligible for something is able or allowed to do or receive it. As paraphrased in the statement, this program "was *intended* to help kids from low-income families".

[①] CATTI (China Accreditation Test for Translators and Interpreters) is the official accreditation test for interpreters in China.

Example 2:

AUDIO: "Consider three major recent California earthquakes: Loma Prieta in 1989, with a 6.9 magnitude, Northridge in 1994, with a 6.7 magnitude, and San Simeon/Paso Robles on December 22, 2003, with a 6.5 magnitude. These relatively strong earthquakes in California resulted in a total of 125 deaths, while this week's Iranian quake, with a somewhat lesser magnitude, claimed 40,000 lives" (卢敏, 2009: 71).

STATEMENT: Such awful losses of human life in the Iranian quake should not have occurred. (True) (卢敏, 2009: 51)

This audio involves the comparison of numbers—it compares the casualties of earthquakes in California with those of another earthquake in Iran, which, though less powerful, causes greater casualties. The implied meaning of this is that, since the earthquake in Iran is less powerful, it should have caused less damage and greater casualties could have been avoided, and thus "should not have occurred".

Example 3:

AUDIO: "The circumstances under which the president left office set a dangerous precedent for democratically elected governments everywhere, as it promotes the unconstitutional removal of duly elected person from office." (卢敏, 2009: 71)

STATEMENT: The removal of the president was a very dangerous and unconstitutional example for other democratic countries. (True) (卢敏, 2009: 52)

The sentence of this audio contains a causal sequence; the reason is in the main clause, and the result is in the subordinate clause, with the two clauses being connected by the conjunction "as". In the statement, "president left office" is paraphrased as "the removal of the president" and "set a ... precedent" is paraphrased as "was ... example".

Chapter Five Reconstruction of the Processing Model of Conference Interpreting

Example 4:

AUDIO: "Most NASA spacecraft rely on some form of chemical propellant to push themselves through space. But at the Marshall-based center, researchers are studying a range of future propulsion methods, including propellant-less systems, simulated fission engines that could one day lead to the real thing and the basic technologies necessary for future antimatter drives." (卢敏, 2009: 29)

STATEMENT: In the future, people may not use chemicals to propel spacecraft. (True) (卢敏, 2009: 7)

The statement mostly concerns the second sentence in the audio, which is a rather long and complex sentence. In the statement, "not use chemicals to propel" paraphrases "propellant-less systems"; thus the statement correctly captures the meaning of the audio. Also, two sentences in the audio have a contrast relation; the second sentence begins with "but", a strong signal that it contains information that contrasts with information coming before it.

Example 5:

AUDIO: "Globalcall Communications has grown from a telecommunications solutions provider for local businesses in the greater Seattle metropolitan area to a truly global corporation providing telecommunications solutions for clients both large and small. Established to fill a significant market gap for simple communication solutions, the company first expanded to most major North American cities before becoming a major multinational player." (卢敏, 2009: 30)

STATEMENT: The company began by offering computer software solutions to local businesses in the greater Seattle metropolitan area. (False) (卢敏, 2009: 7)

The first sentence in the audio is a rather long sentence, though not very complex. It has a simple structure "has grown from ... to ..."; however, the difficulty in understanding this sentence by listening lies in the massive amount of information it contains—a total of seven information units:

$$\text{FROM} \begin{cases} \text{a telecommunications solutions provider;} \\ \text{for local businesses;} \\ \text{in the greater Seattle metropolitan area.} \end{cases}$$

$$\text{TO} \begin{cases} \text{a truly global corporation;} \\ \text{providing telecommunications solutions;} \\ \text{for clients;} \\ \text{both large and small.} \end{cases}$$

Understanding this sentence requires first identifying its information hierarchy (IH) and then remembering the massive information within that hierarchy thereafter. The structure "has grown from ... to ..." is prior to all other massive information.

Such an IH usually becomes a barrier to understanding longer segments though listening, as each level contains massive information. The interpreter must not only understand and remember the various pieces of information, but also analyze the connections among them. To cope with such difficulty involves the second dimension of AL (reflecting), which builds on the first; in other words, the interpreter should first identify the IH and then understand the exact meaning of both the surface and deep structure of each level therein. This is illustrated with examples from Part IV of the English Language Skills Test of Level 2 of CATTI. In this part of the test, candidates listened to a passage once, and then wrote a short summary of around 150–200 words. The passage contained approximately 500 words, so verbatim memorization of the entire passage was impossible within the time limits of the test. To summarize the passage and demonstrate a clear and full understanding thereof, the interpreter had to distinguish between major and minor information and then, after listening, reflect first on the major information, and then back it up with as much minor information as possible.

Chapter Five　Reconstruction of the Processing Model of Conference Interpreting

Example 6:

AUDIO:

"Many people believe that the news is biased in favor of one point of view. During the 1996 presidential campaign, Bob Dole often charged that the press was against him. 'Annoy the Media-Elect Dole' became one of his favorite lines. The charge that the media have a liberal bias has become a familiar one in American politics, and there is some limited evidence to support it. A lengthy study by the Los Angeles *Times* in the mid-1980s found that reporters were twice as likely to call themselves liberal as the general public. A 1992 survey of 1,400 journalists found that 44 percent identified themselves as Democrats, compared to just 16 percent who said they were Republicans.

"However, there is little reason to believe that journalists' personal attitudes sway their reporting of the news. The vast majority of social science studies have found that reporting is not systematically biased toward a particular ideology or party. Most stories are presented in a 'point/counterpoint' format in which two opposing points of view (such as liberal versus conservative) are presented, and the audience is left to draw its own conclusions. A number of factors explain why the news is typically characterized by such political neutrality. Most reporters strongly believe in journalistic objectivity, and those who practice it best are usually rewarded by their editors. In addition, media outlets have a direct financial stake in attracting viewers and subscribers and do not want to lose their audience by appearing biased—especially when multiple versions of the same story are readily available. It seems paradoxical to say the competition produces uniformity, but this often happens in the news business.

"To conclude that the news contains little explicit partisan or ideological bias is not to argue that it does not distort reality in its coverage. Ideally, the news should mirror reality; in practice there are far too many possible stories for this to be the case. Journalists must choose which stories to cover and to what degree. The overriding bias is toward stories that will draw the largest audience. Surveys show that people are most fascinated by stories with conflict, violence, disaster, or scandal. Good news is unexciting; bad news has the drama that brings in big audiences.

"Television is particularly biased toward stories that generate good pictures. Seeing a talking head (a shot of a person's face talking directly to the camera) is boring; viewers will switch channels in search of more interesting visual stimulation. For example, during an unusually contentious and lengthy interview of George Bush by Dan Rather concerning the Iran-Contra scandal, CBS's ratings actually went down as people tired of watching two talking heads argue for an extended period of time. A shot of ambassadors squaring off in a fistfight at the United Nations, on the other hand, will increase the ratings. Such a scene was shown three times in one day on CBS. Not once, though, was the cause of the fight discussed. Network practices like these have led observers such as Lance Bennett to write that 'the public is exposed to a world driven into chaos by seemingly arbitrary and mysterious forces.'" (卢敏, 2009: 34-35)

ANALYSIS:

Major Information:

(1) Many people believe that the news is biased in favor of one point of view. (This is an introduction to the passage.)

(2) However, there is little reason to believe that journalists' personal attitudes sway their reporting of the news. (The word "however" shows a clear contrast, indicating that a point lies within this sentence.)

(3) A number of factors explain why the news is typically characterized by such political neutrality. (This sentence is a subordinate topic.)

(4) To conclude that the news contains little explicit partisan or ideological bias is not to argue that it does not distort reality in its coverage. (This is another point of this passage.)

(5) Television is particularly biased toward stories that generate good pictures. (This is also a

Chapter Five Reconstruction of the Processing Model of Conference Interpreting

point of this passage.)

Corresponding Minor Information (italicized words and phrases are key words of minor information):

(1) *The charge that* the media have a *liberal bias* has become a familiar one in American politics, *and there is* some limited *evidence* to support it. (This sentence summarizes the previous examples to show the author's opinion.)

(2) −1 *Studies have found that* reporting is not *systematically* biased toward a particular *ideology* or party.

(2) −2 Most stories are presented in a "*point/counterpoint*" format. (The use of research findings to support the author's opinion is an important part of the argument.)

(3) −1 Most reporters strongly *believe in journalistic objectivity*, and those who practice it best *are* usually *rewarded by* their editors.

(3) −2 *In addition*, media *outlets* have a direct financial *stake* in attracting viewers and subscribers and do not want to lose their audience by appearing biased. (Supporting details make the argument more solid.)

(4) −1 *Journalists must* choose which stories to *cover* and to what *degree*.

(4) −2 The overriding bias is toward stories that will draw the largest audience. (Further exposition on the major point.)

(4) −3 *Good news is* unexciting; *bad news has* the *drama* that brings in big audiences. (Conclusion of the major point.)

(5) −1 Seeing a talking head (a shot of a person's face talking directly to the camera) is boring; viewers will switch channels *in search of* more interesting *visual stimulation*. (Detailed exposition of the major point.)

(5) −2 The public *is exposed to* a world driven into *chaos* by seemingly *arbitrary and myste-*

rious forces. (This is a conclusion of the major point, which is also quoting the authority. It is convincing to use such utterance in the argument.)

SUMMARY CRITERIA:

The summary of the passage should cover ALL five major information pieces and at least FIVE out of the ten minor information pieces (卢敏, 2009: 15). These criteria clearly show the relationship between identifying IH and remembering massive information, i.e., the relationship between two dimensions of AL. In AL, the interpreter should first identify the IH, and then understand and remember the information accordingly.

AL involves not only listening to the interpreter's passive language, but also listening to his/her native language as well. This kind of listening is completely different from that involved in foreign language teaching and learning. The top concern for listening in the interpreting process is to receive all the information and make the communication flow smoothly. The following example is from a press conference in China.

Example 7:

深圳大运会组委会副主席、教育部副部长郝平:

尊敬的各位新闻媒体的朋友们,大家早上好!

深圳第26届世界大学生夏季运动会是继2008年北京奥运会、2010年广州亚运会后我国举办的又一国际综合性体育盛会。本届世界大学生运动会将于8月12日在深圳湾体育中心隆重开幕,届时将有来自180个国家和地区的13000多名运动员及官员参加。运动会共设24个大项,306个小项的比赛。国际大学生体育联合会基里安主席和执委会全体29位执委将出席运动会开幕式。

按照党中央、国务院的总体部署,在广东省委省政府、深圳市委市政府的直接领导下,深圳在赛事规划、场馆建设、志愿者服务等各个方面都做了周密安排、精心部署和卓有成效的工作,各项赛办工作进展顺利。本届大运会将生动体现"年轻的城市举办青年盛会"的时代特色,传递和谐、包容、共享文明的价值观,对向世界展示我国改革开放和现代化建设取得的伟大成就,展示我国大学生文明热情、朝气蓬勃、积极向上的精神面貌都具有重要的意义。

教育部作为深圳大运会组委会主席单位之一,高度重视大运会的筹备工作。在体育总局的指导下,目前教育部已经完成了中国大学生体育代表团的组团工作。代表团总人数为804人,其中运动员505人,来自26个省、自治区、直辖市的110所高校,将参加全部24个大项的283个小项比赛。在相关部门的支持与配合下,我们将认真抓好中国代表团的集训和备战工作。在注重大学生运动员的技战术专业训练和体能训练的同时,教育部还会开展体育道德与精神文明教育和赛风赛纪教育,向世界充分展示中国大学生运动员良好的精神风貌和精湛的竞技水平,力争取得精神文明和竞赛成绩双丰收。

本次大运会期间,国际大学生体育联合会将举行换届选举大会,153个会员国家和地区的三百多名代表将出席换届大会。大会将选举产生新一届的国际大学生体育联合会执委会。大运会期间还将组织参赛国的大学校长举办世界大学校长论坛,促进高校及体育界的双边、多边学术合作,积极探索体教结合的新思路,促进与会国家的人文与教育交流。联合国教科文组织总干事波克瓦女士将出席校长论坛开幕式。

现在距离大运会开幕只有21天了,教育部将一如既往地协同中宣部、外交部、体育总局等部门做好宣传、外事、竞赛等各项协调工作,将一如既往地支持、协作深圳市做好最后冲刺阶段的筹备工作。

谢谢大家。

(Briefing on the preparation work for Universiade Shenzhen 2011, State Council Information Office, July 22nd, 2011)

ANALYSIS:

Major Information:

(1) 深圳第26届世界大学生夏季运动会是继2008年北京奥运会、2010年广州亚运会后我国举办的又一国际综合性体育盛会。

（2）深圳在赛事规划、场馆建设、志愿者服务等各个方面都做了周密安排、精心部署和卓有成效的工作，各项赛办工作进展顺利。

（3）教育部作为深圳大运会组委会主席单位之一，高度重视大运会的筹备工作。在体育总局的指导下，目前教育部已经完成了中国大学生体育代表团的组团工作。

（4）本次大运会期间，国际大学生体育联合会将举行换届选举大会。

（5）教育部将一如既往地协同（多部门）做好各项协调工作，将一如既往地支持、协作深圳市做好最后冲刺阶段的筹备工作。

Corresponding Minor Information：

（1）本届世界大学生运动会将于 8 月 12 日在深圳湾体育中心隆重开幕。

（2）本届大运会将生动体现"年轻的城市举办青年盛会"的时代特色。

（3）在相关部门的支持与配合下，教育部将认真抓好中国代表团的集训和备战工作。

（4）大运会期间还将组织参赛国的大学校长举办世界大学校长论坛。

（5）现在距离大运会开幕只有 21 天了。

Examples 5, 6 and 7 show that an IH exists at both the sentence and the discourse level, as shown in Figure 5.4 and Figure 5.5, below：

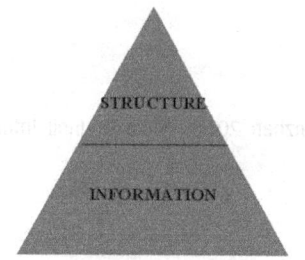

Figure 5.4　Information Hierarchy（IH）at sentence level

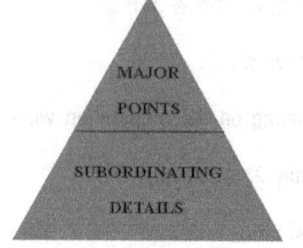

Figure 5.5　Information Hierarchy（IH）at discourse level

Chapter Five Reconstruction of the Processing Model of Conference Interpreting

The hierarchy exists among the information, which is carried by the language. Within a sentence, especially an extreme long or complex sentence, sentence structure ranks higher than information in the IH; within a discourse, especially an exposition or argumentation, major points rank higher than subordinating details. IH also sheds light on other interpreting skills, such as working memory and note-taking, as will be discussed below. To this point, the author has formulated AL in refining comprehension in the processing model.

5.2 Logical Analysis (LA)

As previously discussed, in AL, the interpreter must identify the speaker's IH. According to the *Longman Dictionary of Contemporary English* (2004), a hierarchy is "a system of organization in which people or things are divided into levels of importance". To distinguish information's level of importance according to the speaker's IH, this study uses Logical Analysis (LA). The *Longman Dictionary of Contemporary English* (2004) explains "logical" as "using a thinking process in which facts and ideas are connected in a correct way".

LA is a process in which the interpreter gets to the major points and structure of a discourse by removing the redundant message and adjusting the speaker's original illogical clues. Like active listening, it falls into two dimensions. In the first, the interpreter distinguishes the speaker's logical hierarchy, which is reflected in the IH at the discourse level. After listening to a speaker's discourse, the interpreter should be able to generalize the topic of thereof within one sentence, which is at the very top of the IH; then, the interpreter should list the major points of this topic, which are at the second level of the IH, before going on to the subordinating details of each major point, which form the next IH level. In this way, the message of a discourse is separated into different levels, showing a hierarchy of logic.

The second dimension involves determining the logical connections within the message, which are usually reflected in the organization of its main points. According to Professor Stephen E. Lucas❶ (2005), the most often used patterns of ordering information by public speakers are: chronological order; spatial order; causal order; problem-solution order; and topical order (Lucas, 2005: 206-211). The interpreter should recognize the pattern used by the speaker, and then follow that pattern to memorize the points and details accordingly. The following are examples of each of the five patterns:

Example 8:

(LA of a discourse that follows a chronological order.)

吴佳梁：下面我们将分成以下几部分对案子发生的背景、问题的来源、我们的诉求、事件可能的影响和我们的看法向各位做一个说明，再次谢谢各位的光临和倾听。

第一部分，项目背景的相关情况说明。项目背景、项目地点与相关情况。

Butter Creek 项目位于美国俄勒冈州西南12英里处，该项目包括四个独立的风电组成，本项目与附近的项目共享，已获得并网协议、FAA 等所有的合法手续。

---

❶ Stephen E. Lucas is Professor of Communication Arts and Evjue-Bascom Professor in the Humanities at the University of Wisconsin-Madison. He has directed the introductory public speaking course at the University of Wisconsin-Madison since 1973. In 2002, he served as a judge at China's national collegiate English-language public speaking competition, which was sponsored by Ericsson and 21st *Century*.

Chapter Five Reconstruction of the Processing Model of Conference Interpreting

今年2月28日，美国Ralls公司❶与希腊电网公司Terna US签订资产收购合同，Ralls公司正式收购Terna US公司美国俄勒冈州Butter Creek的风场项目，我们取得了项目建设融资，并开发与中国民营房地产企业就项目建成后的转让展开谈判。4月，项目公司与美国当地知名建筑商签订合同，由这个公司负责项目建设，我方派出人员作为项目监理，负责项目建设管理、进度协调等工作。

5月，美国海军西北舰队以Butter Creek项目中一个风场可能影响其空军训练为由，与三一交涉迁址事宜。尽管美国海军无权审批风场建设和空域管理，而相关项目已于2010年9月取得美国联邦航空管理局颁发的"无潜在危险"许可，Ralls仍配合同意将其风场南移了1.5英里。为此，美国海军出具了专门的支持函帮助Ralls再次申请FAA许可并对Ralls的配合表示感谢。

6月14日告知三一：其已接到国防部通知，该项目受到CFIUS❷关注。Ralls集团根据规定对项目进行披露，要求我们提交报告。我们聘请了专业律师，并由6月28日提供了项目交易相关报告，7月11日在华盛顿就Butter Creek项目举行专门听证会。

7月25日CFIUS以涉嫌国家安全为由发出临时命令，要求我们立即停工，禁止存放或堆存任何设备，立即移走全部设备包括已经浇筑的基础环等。禁止任何人进入，只允许CFIUS同意的美国人进入移走设备。

在我方得到禁令并试图将项目转让给美国人持有的美国公司以减少损失时，8月2日，CFIUS又颁布了临时禁令和修改令。追加了两点：一、该项目禁止使用三一设备；二、该

---

❶ Ralls Corp. is a Delaware-registered company controlled by SANY.
❷ The Committee on Foreign Investment in the United States (CFIUS) is an inter-agency committee authorized to review transactions that could result in control of a U. S. business by a foreign person ("covered transactions"), in order to determine the effect of such transactions on the national security of the United States. In this lawsuit, Ralls argued that CFIUS acted in an arbitrary manner by ordering the company to cease construction at its wind farms without revealing what the national security concerns were, or how they could be addressed.

项目禁止转让直到所有设备移除完毕,且告知 CFIUS 买方信息 10 个工作日内未被 CFIUS 拒绝。

大家看这个图,这里没有任何标志是军事区。这个绿色是已经建成的风场,其中有 27 台为丹麦的风机,区域内还有已经运行的风场。

这是美国太平洋电力公司所有的电厂的规模,上表为已经接入太平洋电力公司的项目。项目开工建设前得到了专业团队的确认,全部手续完整合法。

(*Introduction to the questioned Butter Creek Project*, SANY Group's U. S. Wind Farm Lawsuit Media Briefing, October 18th, 2012)

LOGICAL ANALYSIS:

This introduction to the questioned Butter Creek Project formed the first part of a media briefing.

The first dimension of LA is to identify the discourse's IH.

· Central Idea:Butter Creek 的风场项目案件产生过程中的六大事件。

· Main Points:

(1) 2012 年 2 月 28 日,Butter Creek 风场项目正式确立。

(2) 4 月,项目进入具体实施环节。

(3) 5 月,迁址事宜提出,风场南移 1.5 英里。

(4) 6 月 14 日,获悉该项目受到 CFIUS 关注,7 月 11 日举行听证会。

(5) 7 月 25 日 CFIUS 发布第一大命令。

(6) 8 月 2 日,CFIUS 又发布第二大命令。

· Subordinating Details:

<1>Butter Creek 项目双方。

<2>项目建设、项目监理的分配。

<3>迁址事宜的提出方、缘由及其结果。

Chapter Five Reconstruction of the Processing Model of Conference Interpreting

<4>Ralls 集团对项目进行披露,三一提交报告。

<5>第一大命令发布的缘由及命令具体要求。

<6>追加命令发布的前提及内容。

The second dimension is to determine its logical connections. Obviously, this introduction follows a chronological order, as signaled by its noting the exact date or time of each event. This connection can be shown in the form of an outline.

Outline:

一、2012 年 2 月 28 日,Butter Creek 风场项目正式确立

    1. Butter Creek 项目是由三一集团的美国子公司 Ralls 公司从希腊电网公司 Terna US 手中收购而得;

    2. 三一取得项目建设融资并开发。

二、4 月,项目进入具体实施环节

    1. 项目建设方为美国当地知名建筑商;

    2. 项目监理为三一集团,负责建设管理、进度协调等工作。

三、5 月,迁址事宜提出,风场南移 1.5 英里

    1. 迁址事宜的提出方为美国海军西北舰队;

    2. 迁址缘由为风场可能影响其空军训练;

    3. 相关项目虽已经取得许可,但依旧南移 1.5 英里。

四、6 月 14 日,获悉该项目受到 CFIUS 关注,7 月 11 日举行听证会

    1. Ralls 集团对项目进行披露;

    2. 三一于 6 月 28 日提交报告。

五、7 月 25 日 CFIUS 发布第一大命令

    1. 命令发布缘由为涉嫌国家安全;

    2. 命令具体要求包括:

(1) 立即停工;

(2) 禁止存放设备;

(3) 立即移走全部设备;

(4) 禁止进入等。

六、8 月 2 日，CFIUS 又发布第二大命令

1. 命里发布前提为三一试图转让项目以减少损失;

2. 命令追加内容包括:

(1) 该项目禁止使用三一设备;

(2) 该项目转让的条件。

Discourses that are organized chronologically usually follow a time sequence, and may refer to a series of sequential events. Note that, in this scenario, the discourse is rather long and contains a great deal of information for the interpreter to remember. LA functions as a facilitator of working memory, which consists of both long-and short-term memory. The psychologist George Miller, in his highly influential article, *The Magical Number Seven, Plus or Minus Two*, suggested that human short-term memory has a forward memory span of approximately seven items, plus or minus two (Miller, 1956), and that information can be stored in short-term memory for less than one minute. An interpreter receives huge amounts of information that is unprocessed; thus, memorizing it is a challenge. As Gile (1995) concluded, working memory "operates primarily on currently 'activated' information from long-term memory" and "has a small storage capacity" (Gile, 1995: 167).

LA helps the interpreter reduce the speaker's message from a long discourse to

Chapter Five Reconstruction of the Processing Model of Conference Interpreting

only a few sentences or key words. In the following example, the original discourse contained 893 words, while the outline used only 407; LA reduced the discourse to less than half of its original length.

Example 9:

(LA of a discourse that follows a spatial order.)

这次人口普查,东部地区人口占31个省(区、市)常住人口的37.98%,中部地区占26.76%,西部地区占27.04%,东北地区占8.22%。

与2000年人口普查相比,东部地区的人口比重上升2.41个百分点,中部、西部、东北地区的比重都在下降。其中,西部地区下降幅度最大,下降1.11个百分点;其次是中部地区,下降1.08个百分点;东北地区下降0.22个百分点。

按常住人口分,排在前五位的是广东省、山东省、河南省、四川省和江苏省。2000年人口普查排在前五位的是河南省、山东省、广东省、四川省和江苏省。

(Figures concerning geographic distribution, taken from a press release on major figures in the 2010 National Population Census, April 28th, 2011)

LOGICAL ANALYSIS:

This discourse, the eighth part of a longer press release, introduced figures relating to the geographic distribution of China's population. Since this discourse contained mainly numbers and their corresponding geographic area and variations, it was better to conduct the two dimensions of LA together; this reduces the analytic workload and guarantees correct numbers.

· Central Idea:我国的人口按照地理位置划分为四大地区。

· Main Points:

(1) 东、中、西、东北四大地区人口百分比。

(2) 与2000年相比,四大地区人口变化情况。

(3) 与 2000 年相比，常住人口排名前五位省份的变化。

· Subordinating Details：

<1>东部：37.98%，+2.41%

<2>中部：26.76%，—1.08%，降幅第二位

<3>西部：27.04%，—1.11%，降幅最大

<4>东北：8.22%，—0.22%，

<5>常住人口：粤、鲁、豫、川、苏

　　2000 年：豫、鲁、粤、川、苏

Discourses organized spatially usually follow a directional sequence, i.e., right to left, bottom to top, north to south, etc. Whatever the route chosen, the interpreter need only keep pace with the speaker, and analyze the message while jotting the numbers down.

Example 10：

(LA of a discourse that follows a causal order.)

多年来，三一高端团队一直在做美国的义务宣传员，广为宣传美国良好的投资环境，这一切表明我们对美国完全是美好的初衷，对美国有极大的热情，我们没有理由做美国国家安全的事情，我再次声明损害美国的国家安全利益就是损失了我们的利益，CFIUS 让我们既损失了金钱也损失了名誉，这是我们无论如何都接受不了的。

CFIUS 制造的 Ralls 冤案会给美国带来什么？今年 7 月 11 日我在华盛顿参加了 CFIUS 的听证会后，作为演讲嘉宾代表三一出席了 7 月 18 日由中美双方共同组织在北京召开的近千名中国企业家参加的促进中美直接投资的论坛。面对数百名参会并有意到美国投资的中国企业家，因为刚刚参加完 CFIUS 的听证会，我以过来人的身份，向与会者热情介绍了大

Chapter Five   Reconstruction of the Processing Model of Conference Interpreting

家普遍关心的 CFIUS 困惑。我告诉我的同胞们，CFIUS 是一个温情的、讲理的、透明的政府机构，到美国投资不必担心 CFIUS 的问题，结果 CFIUS 的大棒就落在了我们的头上。我想我们所受到的对待，对那些准备那些含辛茹苦到美国投资的企业家的信心是何等严重的打击。也许明年我还会是一年一度召开的这个会议的演讲嘉宾，面对这些企业家我又应该说什么？我还能说什么？我很希望 CFIUS 的官员能够告诉我答案。

美国是一个商业立国的国家，工商业强大是美国强大的根本。今天也许美国足够强大，但如果这些莫须有的冤案一再发生，会让所有外来资本都感到没有任何安全感，感觉政府操作的任意性、随意性和不确定性的时候，这恐怕不是美国社会之福，也不是美国民众之福。

小小的一个 Butter Creek 的事件牵动的是数以千计准备到美国投资的中国企业家的心，牵动的是全球成千上万企业家对美国投资的信心。我相信处理不当它将让美国人民丧失数以万计甚至十万计的工作机会。当某些政客可能还在扬扬得意他们的杰作又一次打击了中国时，他们是否会想到制造这些冤案动摇的却是美国的国本和基石。

(*How would Ralls' Lawsuit impact US*, SANY Group's U. S. Wind Farm Lawsuit Media Briefing, October 18th, 2012)

LOGICAL ANALYSIS：

This discoursewas the fifth part of the media briefing.

The first dimension ofLA is to identify the discourse's IH.

· Central Idea：CFIUS 制造的 Ralls 冤案或将使美国的投资环境受到质疑。

· Main Points：

(1) CFIUS 制造了针对三一集团及其美国子公司 Ralls 公司的冤案。

(2) CFIUS 制造的 Ralls 冤案会给美国带来三方面的恶劣影响。

· Subordinating Details：

<1>三一没有理由损害美国国家安全。

<2>三一对 CFIUS 的做法表示无法接受。

<3>Ralls 冤案严重打击了准备到美国投资的企业家的信心。

<4>如果类似冤案一再发生，受害者不仅是美国社会，还有美国民众。

<5>诸如 Butter Creek 事件这类冤案动摇的是美国的国本和基石。

The second dimension is to determine its logical connections. Discourses following a causal order contain two main points—one dealing with the causes, the other with the effects thereof. This discourse places the cause in the first main point and the effects in the second. This dimension of analysis should first separate cause from effects, and then back up each main point accordingly with details. Still, an outline can show their connections.

Outline:

一、CFIUS 制造了针对三一集团及其美国子公司 Ralls 公司的冤案

  1. 三一没有理由损害美国国家安全；

  2. 三一对 CFIUS 的做法表示无法接受。

二、CFIUS 制造的 Ralls 冤案会给美国带来三方面的恶劣影响

  1. Ralls 冤案严重打击了准备到美国投资的企业家的信心；

  2. 如果类似冤案一再发生，受害者不仅是美国社会，还有美国民众；

  3. 诸如 Butter Creek 事件这类冤案动摇的是美国的国本和基石。

In this example, LA helped to reduce the original 717 word discourse to a 155 word outline, which could greatly improve the efficiency of working memory in the interpreting process. The interpreter could take matters a step further and annotate the outline using unique note-taking techniques, so as to stay more focused on the speaker's theme and major points.

Chapter Five Reconstruction of the Processing Model of Conference Interpreting

Example 11:

(LA of a discourse that follows a problem-solution order.)

中新社记者：您好，我们知道这次神舟九号的时间比其他的载人飞行时间都要长，而且还有中国首位女航天员，太空环境对于航天员的不利影响有哪些呢？谢谢。

武平：针对神舟九号任务飞行时间较长的特点，为了保障航天员健康，对抗失重环境对航天员健康的不利影响，我们重点采取了三个方面的措施。

一是采取了新的医学监测和保障措施。在前三次载人飞行中主要是监测航天员心电、血压、体温和呼吸。这次任务增加了航天员的心肺功能和生化等更多医学指标的在轨监测。此外，增配了相关药物和医学保障用品，将定期进行舱内卫生学处理，以确保对航天员健康状况的及时监测和对空间运动病等的有效预防。

二是采取了失重防护的相关措施。失重环境对航天员的心血管系统和肌肉、骨骼系统均会带来不利的影响。为了对抗这种影响，维护航天员的健康，在飞行中，新增了自行车功量计、企鹅服、套带等对抗防护和锻炼用品，以此来维持航天员心血管和肌肉功能，确保航天员保持良好的健康状况和工作状态。

三是采取了对女航天员的针对性措施。针对女航天员的生理特点，在医学检查、锻炼防护等方法上制定专项措施，在飞行程序设计、生活照料安排等方面充分考虑女性需求，以保障她们的健康。

虽然我们采取了上述措施，但是航天员在经过较长时间的失重飞行，再次返回地面后，会不同程度出现立位耐力下降的现象，需要一个重力再适应的过程。因此当航天员返回地面出舱以后出现不能站立的时候大家不要担心，这都是正常的现象。谢谢。

(Press conference on China's manned rendezvous & docking mission inspace, between the Tiangong I space module and the Shenzhou IX spaceship, June 15th, 2012)

LOGICAL ANALYSIS:

This discourse is the quoted from the Q & A section of the press conference.

The first dimension of LA is to identify the discourse's IH.

· Central Idea：太空环境对于航天员健康有不利影响，为了保障航天员健康，我们重点采取了三个方面的措施。

· Main Points：

(1) 神舟九号任务的失重环境对航天员健康的有不利影响。

(2) 针对这些影响，采取了医学监测保障、失重防护和相应的针对性措施。

· Subordinating Details：

<1>神舟九号的时间比其他的载人飞行时间都要长，而且还有中国首位女航天员。

<2>此次神九任务在医学监测与保障用品的配置多于前三次载人飞行。

<3>此次神九任务新增了对抗失重影响防护和锻炼用品。

<4>针对女航天员的生理特点，充分考虑女性需求。

<5>航天员返回地面出舱以后出现不能站立是正常的现象。

The second dimension involves determining the discourse's logical connections. Discourses following a causal order can be easily divided into two parts—the first showing that a problem(s) exists, the second offering workable solutions. Their connections can be shown using an outline.

Outline：

一、神舟九号任务的失重环境对航天员健康的有不利影响

    1. 神舟九号的时间比其他的载人飞行时间都要长；

    2. 中国首位女航天员。

二、针对这些影响，采取了医学监测保障、失重防护和相应针对性措施

    1. 此次神九任务在医学监测与保障用品的配置多于前三次载人飞行；

    2. 此次神九任务新增了对抗失重影响防护和锻炼用品；

    3. 航天员返回地面出舱以后出现不能站立是正常的现象。

Chapter Five   Reconstruction of the Processing Model of Conference Interpreting

Example 12:

(LA of a discourse that follows a topical order.)

三、关于红十字会的改革创新

《意见》❶提出了三方面要求：一是要建立与社会主义市场经济体制和国际人道主义原则相适应的体制机制，强调通过改革和完善红十字会内部治理结构，创新管理模式，强化民主决策机制，提高组织执行能力等措施，探索建立"高效、透明、规范"的管理体制和运行机制。二是要求各级红十字会按照规定严格执行信息公开制度，做到资金募集、财务管理、招标采购、分配使用等捐赠信息的公开透明，切实保障捐赠人和社会公众的知情权、监督权。同时，要求将红十字会的信息化建设纳入各地信息化建设总体规划，通过信息化手段着力打造公开透明的红十字会。三是全面建立综合性监督体系，强调要建立和完善法律监督、政府监督、社会监督、自我监督相结合的综合性监督体系。同时，要求监察、审计部门加强对红十字会的监察、审计，要建立绩效考评和问责机制，严格实行责任追究。

(Introduction to the Opinions of the State Council on the Promotion of Red Cross Cause Development, State Council Information Office, August 2nd, 2012)

LOGICAL ANALYSIS:

This discourse is taken from the third part of the introduction.

The first dimension of LA is to identify the discourse's IH.

· Central Idea:《意见》对红十字会的改革创新提出三方面要求。

· Main Points:

(1) 对体制机制建设的要求。

(2) 对信息公开制度的要求。

---

❶ 《国务院关于促进红十字事业发展的意见》

(3) 对监督体系建立的要求。

• Subordinating Details：

<1>与社会主义市场经济体制和国际人道主义原则相适应。

<2>目标是"高效、透明、规范"。

<3>做到捐赠信息公开、透明。

<4>将其纳入各地信息化建设总体规划。

<5>建立综合性监督体系。

<6>建立绩效考评和问责机制。

The second dimension is to determine its logical connections. Discourses following a topical order can be divided into several subtopics. Note that the key to the second dimension of LA, in this instance, is the correspondence between subordinating details and main points. The following is an outline for this discourse.

Outline：

一、《意见》对红十字会体制机制建设的要求

  1. 与社会主义市场经济体制和国际人道主义原则相适应；

  2. 目标是"高效、透明、规范"。

二、对信息公开制度的要求

  1. 做到捐赠信息公开、透明；

  2. 将其纳入各地信息化建设总体规划。

三、对监督体系建立的要求

  1. 建立综合性监督体系；

  2. 建立绩效考评和问责机制。

Up until now, the author has specified Logical Analysis (LA) when refining analysis in the processing model of conference interpreting. In these examples of LA, an outline can show the order of the discourse's main points and the organization of its subordinating details with a clear simplicity of style. Examples 8 and 10 also shed light on another important issue-working memory. LA helps the interpreter to better process information by making it more concise and accessible. Working memory is discussed further in the following section.

5.3 Register Preparation (RP)

The third aspect to be studied is working memory. Conference interpreters trigger their short- and long-term memory as working memory. As discussed in section 2.3 of this study, numerous researchers have addressed the issue of short-term memory. Given that the aim of this study is to refine the processing model for conference interpreting, its discussion of working memory focuses on what previous processing models seldom mention long-term memory.

In the interpreting process, the interpreter does not receive the message mechanically, but comprehends it through AL. Long-term memory allows the interpreter access to linguistic knowledge and extra-linguistic knowledge with which to process the massive information, and thus facilitates the more effective use of short-term memory. In other words, long-term memory is a storehouse of knowledge that the interpreter triggers and activates, so as to transfer knowledge from the discourse to his/her short-term memory more quickly. To ensure the activeness of long-term memory, the interpreter must stimulate its stored knowledge constantly.

In actual conference interpreting practice, the theme and subject covered in each conference vary, and an experienced conference interpreter has stored, in his/her long-term memory, knowledge about a wide range of different subjects. The interpreting process shown in the Triangular Model starts at the point of comprehension (revised, in this study, as Active Listening); however, that is not the reality of conference interpreting. The conference interpreter is not simply thrust into a conference, and preparation for the task ahead is always needed. This can involve several days of pre-interpreting preparation, or just a few minutes getting briefed on the theme, speakers and other necessary background information. This step cannot and should not be ignored, as the interpreter is be assigned by the organizer to be a part of the conference, and is integral to its success. To ensure the accurate and efficient conduct of the conference, the organizer will always brief the interpreter with information about the speaker and/or topic, even in such scenarios as emergency meetings or talks.

The author of this study thus incorporates pre-interpreting preparation as a trigger and stimulus to long-term memory, making it the real start of the interpreting *process and a facilitator of working memory*. Pre-interpreting preparation has a dual target—to activate the relevant linguistic and extra-linguistic knowledge stored in long-term memory, and to complement them from the scenario. This dual target requires the prediction and preparation of the interpreter's register.

The concept of "register" was formulated by Halliday and Hasan, in 1976, in their book *Cohesion in English*, which states that the "linguistic features which are

Chapter Five Reconstruction of the Processing Model of Conference Interpreting

typically associated with a configuration of situational features—with particular values of the field, mode and tenor—constitute a REGISTER." (Halliday & Hasan, 1976: 22) A register is determined by three variables (field, tenor, and mode), variations of which lead to different registers.

Field is the total event that takes place in the communication process. It involves not only the subject-matter (i. e., the topic or theme of communication), such as politics, commerce or legal issues, but also the participants and the entire constellation of activity in the setting. Tenor refers to the interactions among the participants in the communication, and involves a participant's identity, social status, and relationship with other participants. Mode is the function of the discourse in communication, which is reflected in both its language channel (e. g., prepared or impromptu, spoken or written) and its genre (e. g., informative or persuasive).

Halliday (1978) also proposed that register has a predictive function, noting that, if the social context of language use is known, then a great deal of the language that will occur in a given situation can be predicted, and such predictions are reasonably likely to be correct (Halliday, 1978: 31–35). This function corresponds with the dual targets of pre-interpreting preparation. By analyzing the three concepts of register, the interpreter can prepare for a conference's theme, context, language channel and genre, the relations among its participants, and even (to a degree) its message. Thus, proper pre-interpreting preparation should include three aspects: field preparation, tenor preparation; and mode preparation.

The following are examples for each of the three aspects. The examples are taken from a blog article by AIIC interpreter Zhan Cheng❶, *Interpreting for Jack Welch on the Mid-autumn Day*❷, in which he presents his preparation process for one of his interpreting tasks, a simultaneous interpreting task for the TV program *DIALOG* in CCTV-9, with Jack Welch❸ being the guest. Business talks can be seen a kind of conference activity, so interpreting for this TV program is also conference interpreting in its nature. Zhan Cheng was assigned the task just one day before the TV program, and did his pre-interpreting preparation in accordance with the three aspects mentioned above.

Example 13:

Field Preparation:

"Since the dialog in this program was impromptu, there was no written material for the interpreter. So I got up early and researched information about Jack Welch on the Internet for two hours. The following are my notes:

Chairman and CEO of General Electric 1981—2001

2006, net worth $720m.

---

❶ Zhan Cheng is currently an associate professor at Guangdong University of Foreign Studies (GDUFS) and vice-dean of School of Interpreting and Translation Studies at GDUFS. In 2011, he was invited by the 21st Century to write a blog for the i21st. cn. This example is cited from one of his blog entries at http: //home. i21st. cn/space-284507. html

❷ Excepting the notes in Example 13, all citations from the blog were translated by the author of this study.

❸ Jack Welch was chairman and CEO of General Electric from 1981–2001, and is the second most admired Western businessman among Chinese businessmen, the first being Bill Gates. His autobiography, *Winning*, is considered the Bible for business management in China.

Chapter Five Reconstruction of the Processing Model of Conference Interpreting

Born Salem, Massachusetts

父: Boston & Maine Railroad conductor

母: homemaker

妻: Carolyn, Jane, Suzy

Univ. of Ma. Amherst

BS Chemical Engineering

Phi Sigma Kappa Fraternity

MS & PhDUniv. of Illinois at Urbana-Champaign

加入 GE 1960

VP 1972, Senior VP 1977, VC 1979

"Growing Fast in a Slow-growth Economy" (1981 NYC), the dawn of the obsession with shareholder value

Brutal candor-reward top 20%; fire bottom 10%

Neutron Jack 中子弹杰克

Croton vile 管理学院

Eliminated 9-layer management hierarchy

1990s GE 转型 manufacturing → financial services

Motorola's Six Sigma quality program 1995

GE most valuable and largest company

"Manager of the Century" by *Fortune Magazine*

继任: Jeffrey Immelt

Excessive CEO pay

Lack of compassion for middle and working class

2005 book "Winning"

· *109* ·

4E 理论: energy, energizing, edge, execute

新 4E: empathy, experimental, example, excited

活力曲线 271"

(Taken from Zhan Cheng's blog: *Interpreting for Jack Welch on the Mid-autumn Day*)

This was Zang Cheng's field preparation. The entire event was a TV program, with the subject-matter or theme being an interview with Jack Welch. Such programs usually focus on business or political tycoons, presenting their ideas and giving them context by reviewing their family, background, experience and achievements. The host's aim was to present the celebrity guest's experience to the audience by leading the guest to recount his own stories. Thus, the aim of the interpreter was to represent the guest's own telling of his story in the target language, and also to represent the host's questions that informed the flow of the dialog. Zhan Cheng's note covers the following topics:

① Jack Welch's Family / Hometown

② Education / University / Degrees

③ Career / Position / Fields of Business

④ Achievements and Titles

⑤ Managing ideas

These topics have been previously covered by various media and could be accessed over the Internet. Having the guest's information is important; it is like having access to some of the guest's major information ahead of the dialog. Having this in mind makes identifying the source message's IH and LA easier, as the interpreter need merely complement major information with supporting details, already at hand. The interpreter can even predict the story to be told by the guest himself. This is the function of REGISTER.

Chapter Five   Reconstruction of the Processing Model of Conference Interpreting

Example 14:

Tenor Preparation:

"I often watch *Dialog*. On the program, they often invite business tycoons to talk about business and commerce. It is a very interactive program, for there is often an impromptu Q & A session during the interview. This task is much more difficult than interpreting for a seminar or a forum. The frequent interaction requires the interpreter to respond instantly; any hesitation could break the flow of the dialog. In addition, such circumstances are very challenging for the interpreter. Any mistakes on the part of the interpreter could lead to misunderstandings between the interviewer and the interviewee, and the audiences would immediate know that something went wrong with the interpreter."

(Take from Zhan Cheng's blog: *Interpreting for Jack Welch on the Mid-autumn Day* and translated by the author of this study)

Tenor refers to who is taking part in the event. Since this program was going to be on TV and could include an impromptu question and answer session, the dialog to be interpreted was not just between host and guest. Participants in this activity could be divided into three groups:

① Participant A-Host-Chen Weihong

② Participant B-Guest-Jack Welch

③ Participant C-Audience-Studio Audience and TV Audience

The host led the dialog, as he triggered new topics by probing into the guest's story. The guest was the center of communication, as his story was what the audience wanted to hear. Though the audience did not participate directly in the dialog, they could be rather active in this activity, as their response is an important criterion for the success of interview. If an audience cannot following the pace set by the host and guest, they know that something must have gone wrong with the interpreting. Usually, whenever interpreting is mentioned, the speaker and the listener are involved; in this case, however, a third party (the audience) is also involved, making the interpreter a coordinator of and catalyst for cross-cultural communication.

Example 15:

Mode Preparation:

"Interpreting for Jack Welch? The former CEO of General Electric, with a reputation as the best CEO in the world? The man who pumped GE's stock market value from $13 billion when he took over to $560 billion today? I still remember several years ago, when his autobiography *Winning* was published in China, it was regarded as the managing Bible for numerous entrepreneurs."

"When my partner and I arrived at the studio, we got a document from the TV program, outlining the purpose and background of the program, the recording process in the studio, scripts for the voice-over and the host, as well as preparatory questions etc. Having this in hand, we immediately buried ourselves in the booth and read it thoroughly."

(Taken from Zhan Cheng's blog: *Interpreting for Jack Welch on the Mid-autumn Day* and translated by the author of this study)

Mode refers to the function of the discourse, and is reflected in both its language channel and its genre or rhetorical mode. Both spoken and formal language were used on the TV program to present the guest's story, ideas and thoughts to the audience. Thus the rhetorical mode of the language in this case can be seen as narrative (when the guest was telling his own story) and didactic (when he was sharing his managerialideas). Since the interpreter had watched previous episodes of the program, he immediately recognized that the difficulty of this task lay in the interaction among the participants, which could be unpredictable.

Another challenge for an interpreter in such a situation is that dialog can flow

Chapter Five Reconstruction of the Processing Model of Conference Interpreting

very rapidly between host and guest, and the interpreter must ensure that the audience can follow that flow. Casual spectators may not be able to follow the guest as well as the host can, so the interpreter must be aware of audience responses at all times. By bearing this purpose and relationship in mind, an interpreter can arrange his efforts more reasonably to ensure successful interpreting.

Examples 13, 14 and 15 show that pre-interpreting preparation can be done even for impromptu talks, as the content, language and delivery of the talk can be predicted in accordance with the theory of register.

These three examples, taken together, illustrate pre-interpreting preparation for one form of conference interpreting—interpreting for business talks. Applied in a broader sense, pre-interpreting preparation for conference interpreting can also be conducted in accordance with the theory of register. Thus, this study proposes register preparation (RP) as a substitute for pre-interpreting preparation, as the former more specifically indicates the exact preparations needed in the generalized "pre-interpreting preparation" process. This study incorporates RP into the interpreting process, as the beginning of that process.

RP's three preparation phases (field, tenor and mode) may overlap one another. Putting it more practically, RP covers aspects that can reflect the field, tenor and mode of a given interpreting situation. RP can activate and implement the knowledge needed for comprehension in the interpreter's long-term memory. Since working memory consists of both long-memory and short-term memory, this is usually the starting point of the interpreting process, as the interpreter has already begun to store knowledge and reconstruct the expected message according to his predictions. When the speaker begins to speak, the interpreter's long-term memory has already been activated, so he/she can more easily follow the flow of the speaker's major points and spare more efforts to cover as much subordinating details as possible.

In this section, the author has used RP, a working memory facilitator, in reconstructing the processing model for conference interpreting, and has extended the interpreting process by beginning it at the register preparation stage.

5.4 Knowledge Supplement (KS)

The previous sections have described the interpreting process as beginning with register preparation and then moving on to active listening and logical analysis. The seemingly last step for the interpreter is the re-expression of the message in the target language.

However, inactual conference interpreting practice, individual conferences' themes and purposes vary greatly, meaning that the register differs for each conference. Once the interpreter comprehends the message by using linguistic and extra-linguistic knowledge, re-expression of that message in another language is not a great challenge. However, the interpreter can get stuck in the re-expression process, mostly due to an inability to comprehend certain messages. Such comprehension obstacle susually lead to an extreme condition in which the interpreter does not even know how to explain the message.

Although in the previous discussion, the author proposed using RP, AL, and

Chapter Five Reconstruction of the Processing Model of Conference Interpreting

LA to facilitate comprehension and memorization the message, the interpreter's extra-linguistic knowledge or coordination may not always be enough to cover everything in the discourse that needs to be interpreted. No matter how well an interpreter has prepared—in terms of both linguistic knowledge of the two languages involved and necessary extra-linguistic knowledge—it is always difficult to re-express the message "in its entirety" in the target language.

However, the interpreter can supplement his/her knowledge during the conference interpreting process. For consecutive interpreting, when confronting with an unfamiliar term or uncertainties of comprehension, the interpreter may ask the speaker to clarify, explainor repeat his/her remarks; for simultaneous interpreting, the interpreter may substitute an unfamiliar term with its hyponym or hypernym. Given the flow of the conference, the interpreter may be able to guess the meaning of the term by considering the context in which it was offered. Of course, there are many other ways for the interpreter to determine the exact meaning of certain terms during the interpreting process, but the interpreter must ensure that using these does not affect the flow of the conference. Once the interpreter understands the meaning of an unfamiliar term, it immediate becomes part of his/her knowledge base, and can be utilized in subsequent interpreting processes; this method of supplementing knowledge during the interpreting process is common to almost every interpreter.

The following examples, taken from actual conference interpreting practice, show how the interpreter supplemented his/her knowledge during the interpreting process.

Example 16:

This example is taken from a blog article, by AIIC interpreter Zhan Cheng, reviewing an interpreting task in which the conference participant helped him with the exactness of technical terms. In this example, the Ambassador Extraordinary and Plenipotentiary of Ethiopia was paying a visit to Guangdong Province, and was being introduced at a meeting of the Guangdong Provincial Department of Foreign Trade and Economic Cooperation. Consecutive interpreting was used in this conference, with Zhan Cheng being the conference interpreter.

(Q & A session)

Lady: "尊敬的大使阁下，我知道贵国有很丰富的煤炭资源，我想问一下有没有中国的公司在贵国投资焦煤项目？"

Interpreter: "Your Excellency Mr. Ambassador, I know that Ethiopia has abundant COAL resources. Are there any Chinese companies that have invested in this sector?"

(The Ambassador answered briefly about the involvement of Chinese and Indian companies in coal and fertilizer projects in Ethiopia, and the good prospects for investing in these projects.)

Interpreter (whispered to the Ambassador): "I think the lady wants to know something about COKE, a special sector of coal."

Ambassador (confused): "Coal or coke?"

Interpreter: "Coke, a type of coal."

Ambassador's attendant (whispered to the interpreter): "No, not coke. Coal, charcoal."

(The Ambassador then added briefly on this question.)

(Taken from Zhan Cheng's blog, *Is coke a kind of coal? -An Interlude in Interpreting*❶)

---

❶ This example is taken from one of Zhan Cheng's blog entries at http://home.i21st.cn/space-284507.html

Chapter Five   Reconstruction of the Processing Model of Conference Interpreting

Zhan Cheng reviewed this incident in his blog article, including his hesitation and mental process of pondering over the word "焦煤". He remembered it was "coke" in UK English (not to be confused with the soft drink); being uncertain, he could not simply interpret it as "coke".

There are many factors that may influence the quality of interpreting, and the interpreter has to handle them instantly and properly. When confronted by such scenarios in the interpreting process, the last thing one wishes to do is to get stuck on an unfamiliar word or skip over it. Maintaining the flow of the conference is the top priority, even if it means letting go of some minor information. One possible solution (and one adopted by most interpreters) is to use the unfamiliar term's hypernym, a broader semantic field that includes the unfamiliar word (e.g., "color" is a hypernym for "red").

While the Ambassador was answering the question, the interpreter was still thinking of the English word for "焦煤", and was certain that the English word was "coke", Taking into consideration the working conditions (i.e., that he was seated next to the Ambassador), the interpreter decided to amend the word "coal", which he had used before; however, such amendment is impossible in simultaneous interpreting. Clearly, the Ambassador began to get confused, even though the interpreter tried to explain the word. Luckily, the Ambassador's attendant helped out both the interpreter and the Ambassador.

This is a typical example in which the interpreter makes up for or amends his previous interpreting as his understanding of the context and of certain terms deepens throughout the interpreting process. The interpreter used knowledge supplementation to refine his re-expression of the message, and to clarify some specific information. Such knowledge supplementationis immediately available when interpreting subsequent segments.

Example 17:

This example is taken from the press conference for Mo Yan, held in Stockholm on his winning the Nobel Prize for Literature. Consecutive interpreting was adopted in the conference. The conference interpreter was an AIIC interpreter from Sweden.

(Q & A session)

Reporter: How would you describe your friend, your …Goran Malmqvist❶? And what would you do when you get together?

Interpreter: What? How do you describe?

Reporter: Your friend, Goran Malmqvist.

Audience (reminding the interpreter): 马悦然.

Interpreter: Oh, 马悦然, ok. And?

Reporter: And what do you do when you get together? How do you spend your time together?

Host: He is from Sveriges Television.

Interpreter: Ok, 我是, 这个, ok, sorry, 哎呀, 我是……我是瑞典电视台的。您如何描述您的朋友马悦然? 你们在一起的时候都做些什么?

Mo Yan then told the pressa story about sharing three cigarettes with Goran Malmqvist (马悦

---

❶ Professor Nils Göran David Malmqvist (Chinese name 马悦然), is a Swedish linguist, member of the Swedish Academy (Chair No. 5), literary historian, sinologist and translator.

Chapter Five Reconstruction of the Processing Model of Conference Interpreting

然) and described their friendship.

(Press Conference with Mo Yan inStockholm, Capital of Sweden, Dec. 6, 2012)

The obstacle emerged from the interpreter's comprehension of the source language. The Chinese name 马悦然 is known to people whose native language is Chinese; however, his Swedish name, Goran Malmqvist, is completely different from his Chinese name in both spelling and pronunciation. The interpreter did not understand to what or whom the reporter was referring on hearing the words "Goran Malmqvist" and so asked the reporter to repeat the question. The reporter then repeated the name, but the interpreter still showed confusion by her facial expression. Another reporter from the audience understood that the reporter was referring to a Swedish name, and reminded the interpreter that the reporter was actually asking about "马悦然." The interpreter immediately corresponded the Chinese name with the Swedish name, thus improving her understanding of the source language.

When the interpreter began to interpret the reporter's question, she became tongue tied, as she was switching back and forth between English and Chinese unconsciously. However, this minor mistake did not affect the general flow of the conference. Mo Yan understood the sense of the question with the help of the interpreter and the audience, who helped the interpreter out with the key word.

This is a typical example in which the interpreter gets help from other conference participants. In such scenarios, others supplement the interpreter's knowledge, so as to help him/her comprehend the source language. Examples 16 and 17 show that, once the interpreter received supplementary knowledge, he/she immediately absorbed it into his/her own knowledge, and it immediately became available for both the current and subsequent interpreting segments.

This study thus incorporates Knowledge Supplement (KS) into the processing model for conference interpreting. KS has a dual function—to compensate for incomplete comprehension, and to refine re-expression. All of the elements for the reconstruction of the processing model for conference interpreting are now in place.

5.5 The Refined Processing Model for Conference Interpreting

The Refined Processing Model for Conference Interpreting takes a non-linear approach to conference interpreting. Its aim is to reflect the process of conference interpreting within the global context, at a time when conference interpreting is booming in China. It is built on the basis of reconstruction of previous processing models, as some of their components may not reflect the nature of interpreting between Asian and European languages. For example, the components Comprehension and Analysis found in previous models are specified as, or replaced by Active Listening and Logical Analysis. Working Memory and Re-expression are retained in the refined model, as they are major components and indispensable to the interpreting process. Also, Register Preparation and Knowledge Supplement are added to the interpreting process, as facilitators. The reconstructed processing model for conference interpreting is represented in Figure 5.6, below:

Chapter Five Reconstruction of the Processing Model of Conference Interpreting

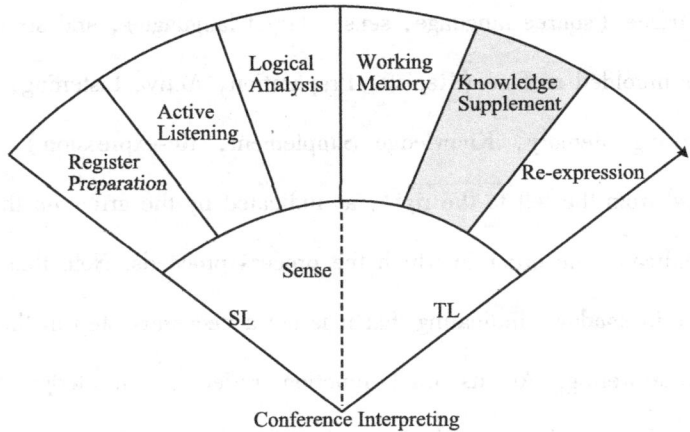

Figure 5.6 **The Refined Processing Model of Conference Interpreting**

The Refined Processing Model of Conference Interpreting takes the form of a traditional Chinese Folding Fan, which resembles a half moon when unfolded. It is also in a "head-gathered" style, as its ends meet when folded. Usually, a Folding Fan's surface is decorated with a painting, calligraphy or poem that is visible when the fan is unfolded and invisible when it is not. In Chinese culture, this decoration usually relates to the owner's or collector's philosophy of life; in Chinese philosophy, the movement of folding and unfolding the fan signifies the veiling and unveiling of one's thoughts.

Inspired by the philosophy underlying the Folding Fan, the process of conference interpreting expands from three basic elements to a group of six components that together constitute the whole process. The Refined Processing Model of Conference Interpreting folding fan consists of three parts: the bottom hinge or pivot point (conference interpreting), three basic elements that give shape to the fan and support its surface (source language, sense, target language), and six components decorating its unfolded surface (Register Preparation, Active Listening, Logical Analysis, Working Memory, Knowledge Supplement, Re-expression). A Folding Fan is unfolded from the left to the right, as indicated by the arrow on the diagram, which also indicates the order in which the process proceeds. Note that Knowledge Supplement is in shadow, indicating that it is not a necessary step in the process of conference interpreting. As its dual function reflects, Knowledge Supplement happens only when the interpreter's comprehension is incomplete, functioning as a polish to the whole process to ensure exactness of re-expression.

5.6 Summary

This chapter has reconstructed the processing model for conference interpreting on the basis of a detailed evaluation of previous models (see Chapter Four). Some of the elements from the previous models have been specified—Active Listening and Logical Analysis are the specifications for Comprehension and Analysis, respectively. New elements—Register Preparation and Knowledge Supplement—have been incorporated into the new model to compensate for the inadequacies of the components, Working Memory and Re-expression. To better illustrate the aforementioned reconstruction work, the Refined Processing Model of Conference Interpreting was proposed. This model takes the form of a traditional Chinese Folding Fan. In addition to the four components formulated in this chapter, Working Memory and Re-expression have been retained in the refined model.

Chapter Six

Conclusion

In China, conference interpreting is a budding profession, and research into conference interpreting is gaining more and more attention. In the preceding chapters, the author has evaluated previous processing models of conference interpreting and proposed a refined processing model. In this chapter, the study's major findings and limitations, as well as suggestions for further research are presented.

6.1 Major Findings

The subject of this study is the various processing models for conference interpreting, the most prevalent of which are Daniel Gile's Effort Models and Lin Yuru's XiaDa Model. As demand for interpreters increases, more and more conference interpreter training programs are being set up in China, and conference interpreting teachers have become a large part of the CIR community. Their research often takes the form of curriculum design, training models and textbooks that have, in turn, refined the processing models. Zhong Weihe's Knowledge Requirements for Interpreters and Roderick Jones' *Conference Interpreting Explained* are two major refinements of existing processing models.

Interpretive Theory was CIR's first dominant theory, and its key concept is the deverbalizaiton of sense. Within the scope of IT, the author has evaluated processing models and their refinements in terms of their major components—comprehension, analysis, working memory and re-expression—that together make up the interpreting process. Based on that evaluation, the author has reconstructed the processing model of conference interpreting.

Reconstruction of a model is not an easy task. The author, adopting an interdisciplinary approach, has brought in and absorbed various concepts from diverse fields within the social sciences, including Gordon's Active Listening (from leadership and management), Chomsky's theory of the deep and surface structures of language, Harris' discourse analysis and Halliday's notion of register (from linguistics), Baddeley and Hitch's notion of working memory (from psychology), Lucas' notions of communication arts and oral language development in Second Language Acquisition, and the Folding Fan (from traditional Chinese philosophy). These concepts are all applicable in CIR, as conference interpreting is a comprehensive communicative activity. Expanding CIR's prevailing linguistics and cognitive psychology approach to this manner has yielded a productive result and the following major findings:

1. A working definition of conference interpreting is proposed, based on an evaluation of extant definitions, from different perspectives.

2. A Refined Processing Model of Conference Interpreting is proposed, based on an evaluation of previous processing models, as interpreting into and from Asian languages requires unique techniques and capabilities. This model uses the image of a traditional Chinese Folding Fan, and has significant implications for conference interpreting in the current global context.

3. Active Listening is proposed to ensure thorough message comprehension, as linguistic and cultural differences between West and East may impede conference interpreters.

4. There exists an Information Hierarchy in the message to be interpreted, at both the sentence and discourse levels. Identification of information hierarchy facilitates the interpreter's comprehension, analysis, memorization and re-expression.

5. Analysisof the previous processing models is specified as Logical Analysis. The discourse analysis used in the XiaDa Model is of questionable merit, as it is mostly applied to written materials. In addition, logical analysis is informed by active listening.

6. To facilitate the interpreter's working memory, Register Preparation is incorporated into the interpreting process, as it offers hints that allow the interpreter to conduct efficient pre-interpreting preparation.

7. Re-expression is retained from the previous processing models, while an additional (albeit optional) element (Knowledge Supplement) is added to ensure smooth and accurate re-expression. Supplementing knowledge usually happens immediately prior to the re-expression stage, when the interpreter has failed to find a cor-

responding expression in the target language or is unable to comprehend the message within its context. It is a make-up element that may polish the result of conference interpreting.

6.2 Limitations

The author recognizes that this study owns several shortcomings, due to the limitations of time and resources. First, this research takes a purely theoretical approach. Although findings are listed above, they need to be tested quantitatively in the field to verify their credibility.

Second, examples of conference interpreting are difficult to collect. Since conference interpreting is an oral work and some interpreter associations (such as the AIIC) may forbid recordings, raw data on conference interpreting, including the course of actual interpretation and interpreter's strategies for coping with emergent problems, are limited to the recollection of the interpreter him/herself.

Third, the model itself is a concentration of a much broader research. Choosing the model as the research question means gathering together many models in a very inclusive and rather macro form of research. Each section of Chapters Four and Five can be specified for further research. The author of this study hopes to supplement it in his future research.

6.3 Suggestions for Future Research

The author recognizes the need to expand upon the findings in this study, and offers three specific avenues for future research. First, although interpreting falls within the humanities field, quantitative research approaches have been increasingly adopted for its study. In future research, more efforts should be made at collecting a data corpus. Second, future researchers should be trained in mathematics, statistics and experiment design, in order to conduct efficient quantitative studies. Third, as CIR is increasingly interdisciplinary, China's CIR community needs to engage in more communication and exchange with other CIR communities around the world, so as to broaden its scope and horizons.

Bibliography

Association Internationale des Interprètes de Conférence (International Association of Conference Interpreters—AIIC). *Advice to Students Wishing to Become Conference Interpreters*[EB/OL]. http://aiic.net/page/56, 2001-09-20/2012-07-27.

AIIC.*Code of Professional Ethics*[EB/OL]. http://aiic.net/page/54, 1999-12-01/2012-06-01.

AIIC.*Conference Interpreting Training Programs: Best Practice* 2010 [EB/OL]. http://aiic.net/page/60, 1999-12-01/2012-07-16.

AIIC.*Community Interpreting*[EB/OL]. http://aiic.net/page/234, 2000-09-10.

AIIC.*How Do We Interpret*[EB/OL]. http://aiic.net/page/1739, 2005-05-21/2012-05-22.

AIIC.*How Interpreters Work*[EB/OL]. http://aiic.net/node/7/how-interpreters-work, 2011-11-28/2012-07-10.

AIIC.*Memorandum Concerning the Use of Recordings of Interpretation at Conferences*[EB/OL]. http://aiic.net/page/58, 1999-12-01/2012-05-22.

AIIC.*Practical Guide for Professional Conference Interpreters* [EB/OL]. http://aiic.net/page/628, 1999-12-01/2012-11-30.

AIIC.*What Is a Conference Interpreter*[EB/OL]. http://aiic.net/page/1469, 2004-04-20.

Baddeley, A. D. & Hitch, G. J. Working Memory [A]. In Bower, G. (ed). *The Psychology of*

Learning and Motivation: *Advances in Research and Theory*, Vol. 8[C]. New York: Academic Press, 1974.

Baker, M.*In Other Words*: *A Coursebook on Translation* [M]. Beijing: Foreign Language Teaching and Research Press, 2004.

Chernov, G. V. *Inference and Anticipation in Simultaneous Interpreting*: *A Probability-prediction Model* [M]. Amsterdam& Philadelphia: John Benjamins Publishing Company, 2004.

Chomsky, N.&Schüützenberger, M.*Topics in the Theory of Generative Grammar*, in *Current Trends in Linguistics*, Vol. 3[C]. Hague: Mouton. 1963.

Choi J. W. The Interpretive Theory of Translation and Its Current Applications [J]. *Interpretation Studies*, 2003(3): 1-15.

Cokely, D.*Interpretation*: *A Sociolinguistic Model* [M]. Bertonsville, MD: Linstok Press, 1992.

Delisle, J.*Translation*: *An Interpretive Approach* [M]. Ottawa: University of Ottawa Press, 1988.

Delisle, J.*Translators through History* [M]. Amsterdam & Philadelphia: John Benjamins Publishing Company, 1995.

Frishberg, N.*Interpreting*: *An Introduction* [M]. Silver Spring, MD: Registry of Interpreters for the Deaf, 1986.

Gerver, D. Empirical Studies of Simultaneous Interpretation: a Review and a Model [A]. In Brislin, R. (ed.).*Translation* [C]. New York: Gardner Press, 1976.

Gerver, D.& Sinaiko, H. W. (eds).*Language Interpretation and Communication* [C]. New York and London: Plenum Press, 1978.

Gile, D. *Basic Concepts and Models for Interpreter and Translator Training* [M]. Amsterdam& Philadelphia: John Benjamins Publishing Company, 1995.

Gile, D. Conference Interpreting [A].*Encyclopedia of Language and Linguistics* (2nd Ed) [Z]. Oxford: Elsevier, 2006(3): 9-23.

Gile, D. The History of Research into Conference Interpreting: a Scientometric Approach [J]. *Target* 12, 2000(2):297-321.

Gile, D.Le modèle d'efforts et l'équilibre d'interprétation en interprétation simultanée [J].*Meta* 30, 1985(1):44-48.

Gile, D. Methodological Aspects of Interpretation (and Translation) Research [J]. *Target* 3,1991(2):153-174.

Gile, D.Methodological Aspects of Interpretation and Translation Research [A]. In Lambert, S.& Moser-Mercer, B. (eds). *Bridging the Gap: Empirical Research in Simultaneous Interpretation* [C]. Amsterdam& Philadelphia:John Benjamins Publishing Company, 1994:39-56.

Gile, D. Opening up in Interpretation Studies [A]. In Snell-Hornby, M., Pöchhacker, F. & Kaindl, K. (eds). *Translation Studies An Interdiscipline* [C]. Amsterdam&Philadelphia:John Benjamins Publishing Company, 1994:149-158.

Gile, D. Scientific Research vs. Personal Theories in the Investigation of Interpretation [A]. In Gran, L. & Tylor, C. (eds).*Aspects of Applied and Experimental Research on ConferenceInterpretation* [C]. Udine:Campanotto Editore, 1990:28-41.

Gonzalez, R., Vasquez, V.& Mikkelson, H. *Fundamentals of Court Interpretation:Theory, Policy and Practice* [C]. Durham, NC:Carolina Academic Press, 1991.

Gordon, T. *Leader Effective Training (L. E. T.)* [M]. New York: The Berkley Publishing Group, 2001.

Gran, L.& Dodds, J. (eds). *The Theoretical and Practical Aspects of Teaching Conference Interpretation* [C]. Udine:Campanotto Editore, 1989.

Halliday, M. A. K.*An Introduction to Functional Grammar* [M]. London:Edward Arnold, 1983.

Halliday, M. A. K. & Hasan,R.*Cohesion in English* [M]. London:Longman, 1976.

Harris, Z. Discourse Analysis [J].*Language* 28, 1952:1-30.

Bibliography

Herbert, J. *The Interpreter's Handbook: How to Become a Conference Interpreter* [M]. Geneva: Georg, 1952.

Jensen, P. A. SI: A Note on Error Typologies and the Possibility of Gaining Insight in Mental Processes [J]. *Meta* 30, 1985(1): 106-113.

Jones, R. *Conference Interpreting Explained* [M]. Shanghai: Shanghai Foreign Language Education Press, 2008.

Lederer, M. *La Traduction Aujourd'hui: Le Modèle Interprétatif* [M]. Paris: Lettres Modernes-Minard, 1994.

Lederer, M. *La Traduction Simultanée —Expérience et Théorie* [M]. Paris: Lettres Modernes-Minard, 1981.

Lederer, M. Simultaneous Interpretation: Units of Meaning and Other Feature [A]. Pochhacker, F. &Shlesinger, M. (eds). *The Interpreting Studies Reader* [C]. London: Routledge, 2002.

Lucas, S. E. *The Art of Public Speaking* (8th Ed) [M]. Beijing: Foreign Language Teaching and Research Press, 2005.

Miller, G. A. The Magical Number Seven, Plus or Minus Two: Some Limits on Our Capacity for Processing Information [J]. *Psychological Review* 63, 1956: 81-97.

Moser-Mercer, B. Simultaneous Interpretation: A Hypothetical Model and Its Practical Application [A]. In Gerver, D. & Sinaiko, H. W. (eds). *Language Interpretation and Communication* [C]. New York: Plenum Press, 1978, 353-368.

Nida, E. A. *Toward a Science of Translation* [M]. Leiden: E. J. Brill, 1964.

Paul, B. & Frank, C. K. Thinking through Language [J]. *Mind & Language* 16, 2001(4): 351-367.

Phelan, M. *The Interpreter's Resource* [M]. Clevedon, Buffalo, Toronto, Sydney: Multilingual Matters Ltd., 2001.

Pöchhacker, F. *Introducing Interpreting Studies* [M]. London & New York: Routledge, 2004.

Pöchhacker, F.& Shlesinger, M. (eds). *The Interpreting Studies Reader* [C]. London: Routledge, Taylor & Francis Group, 2002.

Sartre, J. P. "*What is Literature?*" *and Other Essays* [M]. Cambridge: Harvard University Press, 1988.

Seleskovitch, D. L' Interpretation de Conferences [J]. *Babel* 8, 1962(1): 13-18.

Seleskovitch, D.*Langage, langues et mémoire* [M]. Paris: Minard Lettres Modernes, 1975.

Seleskovitch, D. *Interpreting for International Conferences: Problems of Language and Communication* [M].Translated byDailey, S. &McMillan, N. Washington: PenandBooth, 1978.

Seleskovitch D. & Lederer, M. *Interpréter pour Traduire* [M]. Paris: DidierÉrudition, 1984.

Seleskovitch D. & Lederer, M. *Pédagogie Raisonnée de l'Interprétation* [M]. Paris: DidierÉrudition, 1989.

Seleskovitch, D. Take Care of the Sense and the Sounds will Take Care of Themselves (or Why Interpreting is not Tantamount to Translating Languages) [J]. *The Incorporated Linguist* 16, 1977 (2): 27-33.

Setton, R. *Simultaneous Interpretation: A Cognitive-Pragmatic Analysis* [M]. Philadelphia: John Benjamins Publishing Company, 1999.

Setton, R. Training Conference Interpreters with Chinese—Problems and Prospects [A]. Richard, K. S. & Liu, C. C. *Translation and Interpreting: Bridging East and West*, Vol. 8 [C]. Hawaii: University of Hawaii Press, 1994.

Stenzl, C. From Theory to Practice and from Practice to Theory [A]. In Gran, L. & Dodds, J. (eds).*The Theoretical and Practical Aspects of Teaching Conference Interpretation* [C]. Udine: Campanotto, 1989.

Stenzl, C.*Simultaneous Interpretation: Groundwork toward a Comprehensive Model* [D]. M. A. Thesis. Birkbeck College, University of London, 1983

鲍刚. 口译理论概述[M]. 北京:旅游教育出版社,1998.

蔡小红. 交替传译思维过程与能力发展——对中国法语译员与学生的交替传译活动进行实证性研究[J]. 现代外语,2001(3):276-285.

蔡小红. 口译评估[M]. 北京:中国对外翻译出版公司,2007.

柴明颎,张爱玲. 论口译专能的开发与培养[A]. 柴明颎,张吉良. 口译的专业化道路:国际经验和中国实践[C]. 上海:上海外语教育出版社,2006.

达尼卡·塞莱斯科维奇. 口译技艺——即席口译与同声传译经验谈[M]. 黄为忻,钱慧杰译. 上海:上海翻译出版公司,1992.

达尼卡·塞莱斯科维奇,玛丽雅娜·勒代雷. 口笔译概论[M]. 孙慧双译. 北京:北京语言学院出版社,1991.

达尼卡·塞莱斯科维奇,玛丽雅娜·勒代雷. 口译理论实践与教学[M]. 汪家荣译. 北京:旅游教育出版社,1990.

达尼卡·塞莱斯科维奇,玛丽雅娜·勒代雷. 口译训练指南[M]. 闫素伟,邵炜译. 北京:中国对外翻译出版有限公司,2011.

范守义. 口译、笔译教学理论研究——介绍丹尼尔·嘉尔著《口译与笔译译员培训的基本概念和模式》[J]. 中国翻译,1998(2):46-49.

费尔南德·莫塞. 英语简史[M]. 水天同,刘世沐,金国芬译. 北京:外语教学与研究出版社,1990.

龚龙生. 从释意理论看口译研究[J]. 中国外语,2008(2):80-84.

郭怡军. 口译释意学派在中国的译介与进展[J]. 昆明理工大学学报(社会科学版),2008(2):100-102.

胡庚申. 国际会议交流英语[M]. 北京:高等教育出版社,2000.

柯平,鲍川运. 世界各地高校的口笔译专业与翻译研究机构(上、中、下)[J]. 中国翻译,2002

(4)、(5)、(6).

黎难秋. 中国口译史[M]. 青岛:青岛出版社,2002.

林郁如. 新编英语口译教程[M]. 上海:上海外语教育出版社,1999.

刘和平. 法国释意理论:质疑与探讨[J]. 中国翻译,2006(4):21-26.

刘和平. 口译技巧——思维科学与口译推理教学法[M]. 北京:中国对外翻译出版公司,2001.

刘和平. 口译理论与教学[M]. 北京:中国对外翻译出版公司,2005.

刘和平. 释意学派理论对翻译学的主要贡献——献给达尼卡·塞莱丝柯维奇教授[J]. 中国翻译,2001(4):62-65.

刘宓庆. 当代翻译理论[M]. 北京:中国对外翻译出版公司,1999.

刘宓庆. 文体与翻译[M]. 北京:中国对外翻译出版公司,1985.

卢敏. 英语二级口译考试真题精选[M]. 北京:外文出版社,2009.

玛丽雅娜·勒代雷. 释意学派口笔译理论[M]. 刘和平译. 北京:中国对外翻译出版公司,2001.

梅德明. 高级口译教程[M]. 上海:上海外语教育出版社,2000.

穆雷,王斌华. 国内口译研究的发展及研究走向[J]. 中国翻译,2009(4):19-25.

王斌华. 口译即释意?——关于释意理论及有关争议的反思[J]. 外语研究,2008(5):72-76.

吴冰. 汉译英口译教程[M]. 北京:外语教学与研究出版社,1995.

吴小力. 记者招待会的口译和释意理论——兼谈释意训练[J]. 中国科技翻译,2007(2):81-84.

肖晓燕. 西方口译研究:历史与现状[M]. 外国语,2002(4):71-76.

许钧. 翻译释意理论辨——与塞莱斯科维奇教授谈翻译[J]. 中国翻译,1998(1):9-13.

许钧,袁筱一. 当代法国翻译理论[M]. 南京:南京大学出版社,1998.

许明. 口译认知过程中"deverbalization"的认知诠释[J]. 中国翻译,2010(3):5-11.

颜治强. 世界英语概论[M]. 北京:外语教学与研究出版社,2002.

张德禄. 语域理论简介[J]. 现代外语,1987(4):23-29.

张吉良. 巴黎释意学派口译过程三角模型研究[J]. 外语教学理论与实践,2011(2):74-80.

张吉良. 巴黎释意学派口译理论成就谈[J]. 中国科技翻译,2009(11):16-19.

张吉良. 从研究方法看释意学派和科学研究派的口译研究[J]. 外语研究,2009(4):68-73.

张吉良. ESIT 模式与中国的口译教学[J]. 中国外语,2008(2):91-96.

张吉良. 国际口译界有关巴黎释意学派口译理论的争议及其意义[J]. 外语研究,2010(10):72-78.

张吉良,柴明颎. 国外口译专业概况及其对我国口译办学的启示[J]. 解放军外国语学院学报,2008(6):59-64.

张吉良. 经典的变迁——巴黎释意学派口译办学模式研究[J]. 外语界,2010(2):30-38.

张维为. 英汉同声传译[M]. 北京:中国对外翻译出版公司,1999.

张文,韩常慧. 口译理论研究[M]. 北京:科学出版社,2006.

钟述孔. 实用口译手册(修订版)[M]. 北京:中国对外翻译出版公司,1991.

仲伟合. 口译训练:模式、内容、方法[J]. 中国翻译,2001(2):30-33.

仲伟合,王斌华. 口译研究的"名"与"实"——口译研究的学科理论建构之一[J]. 中国翻译,2010(5):7-12.

仲伟合,王斌华. 口译研究方法论——口译研究的学科理论建构之二[J]. 中国翻译,2010(6):18-24.

仲伟合. 译员的知识结构与口译课程设置[J]. 中国翻译,2003(4):63-65.